Kenji, courtesy of Take On The Day

ABOUT THE AUTHOR

DR. LAURA SCHLESSINGER is a licensed marriage and family therapist and the author of ten *New York Times* bestsellers. The #1 female talk show host in the country, her award-winning radio program is heard on more than 250 stations internationally, XM Satellite Radio, the Armed Forces Network, and is streamed and podcast on her Web site and her YouTube channel. She is a regular columnist for *Newsmax* and the *Santa Barbara News-Press* and a contributor for *Hannity's America*. She lives in southern California with her husband.

Stop Whining,
Start Living

Stop Whining, Start Living

Dr. Laura Schlessinger

HARPER

NEW YORK • LONDON • TORONTO • SYDNEY

HARPER

A hardcover edition of this book was published in 2008 by HarperCollins Publishers.

STOP WHINING, START LIVING. Copyright © 2008 by Dr. Laura Schlessinger. All rights reserved. Printed in the United States of America. No part of this book may be used or reproduced in any manner whatsoever without written permission except in the case of brief quotations embodied in critical articles and reviews. For information address HarperCollins Publishers, 10 East 53rd Street, New York, NY 10022.

HarperCollins books may be purchased for educational, business, or sales promotional use. For information please write: Special Markets Department, HarperCollins Publishers, 10 East 53rd Street, New York, NY 10022.

FIRST HARPER PAPERBACK PUBLISHED 2009.

The Library of Congress has catalogued the hardcover edition as follows:

Schlessinger, Laura
    Stop whining, start living / Laura Schlessinger.—1st ed.
        p. cm.
ISBN 978-0-06-083833-1 1. Self-acceptance. I. Title.
BF575.S37S35 2008
158—dc22

                                                    2007049930

ISBN 978-0-06-083834-8 (pbk.)

09 10 11 12 13 ID/RRD 10 9 8 7 6 5 4 3 2 1

Contents

Preface

I have spent my whole career striving to help people be and do their best and claim joy from the struggle that is life. The irony is that the struggle to be happy has been a lifelong and difficult one for me too. I have come to see this has been a blessing, since my struggles have helped me understand and motivate others, and the helping of others has fed back into my experiencing joy in life.

I have written many books covering just about every aspect of interpersonal and intimate relationships. This book is different. It is about your relationship with yourself and a coming to terms with the limitations of life and acceptance of opportunities for great peace and happiness.

Simply put, you have to decide for whom you are "dancing," through life, and why. Are you still trying to get a mommy or a daddy to love or approve of you? That was my ballet, and it led me to constantly look for new challenges to "prove my worth," with the frustration of never finding what was, ultimately, impossible: love through success.

Are you not "dancing" at all, lest you be criticized or rejected for not dancing well enough? Are you "dancing" with new partners every moment because you crave the feeling of that first touch? Are you "dancing" roughly, stepping on others' feet, hoping to remedy your hurts by delivering even greater ones?

These and more are some of the themes of this book. My goal is that even before you get through the introduction, you'll tear up, let down your guard, and open your heart to the prospect of making your life more of a pleasure to yourself and to others.

Stop Whining,
Start Living

Introduction

You are what you do—first do good, then feel good.

"*There is, I believe, no such thing as unconditional self-acceptance. Those who say so are promulgating a pernicious lie. One must first live a decent, honorable, and productive life. Only then do you get to feel good about yourself. Seeking to heedlessly gratify your desires or impulses of the moment to do things (or fail to do things) your conscience knows to be contrary to your standards of right, worthy, and virtuous behavior is, in a mental, emotional, and spiritual sense, akin to spending capital that you have not earned, and therefore will eventually cause you to feel very negatively . . . about who and what you are. You cannot in the long run eat your cake and have it too. The longer . . . you behave in certain ways, the more it comes to define you, not only to others, but also to yourself.*"

Robert, one of my listeners, sent this to me with a note that said, "Thank you for helping me to learn this lesson of life." It makes me quite proud to read and hear that folks have learned certain values from me that have given their lives some contentment, direction, or purpose. I have long thought that the ultimate meaningfulness of our lives comes from fulfilling our obligations to others.

For most of us, "others" means friends, family, or colleagues. But what if, as in the case of Robert and me, you are total strangers? How does one become obligated to a stranger? Who is a stranger? Is the person behind you in line at the grocery store or gas pump a stranger to whom you owe nothing? Does that mean you are free to take advantage of your opportunity to dominate his or her time and resources, or be otherwise disdainful? Some people seem to get an actual rush from those stolen moments of pseudo-importance and power.

All strangers, though, are people like you. Have you seen the commercial where individuals see strangers doing good deeds, and then in their turn do something for another—and so it keeps going? Not knowing people's names doesn't mean you don't matter to them or they to you. Look at every human being as an opportunity to advance humanity and add something positive to the résumé of your life.

Does that moment's emotional high from the anonymous win of one-upmanship last? No, it generally doesn't. By the time you get home or to work, you're probably in a worse mood. Why? Ugly sentiments breed uglier feelings, and the inevitable downward spiral continues.

Too many people think that feeling good comes from competition, from beating someone else out for something, be it a parking space or an inheritance, or gaining an edge over someone, be they siblings, coworkers, even spouses and children. These are mentalities that drive people deeper into despair because although these "wins" might mean momentary glee, the deeper needs for admiration, love, and respect are never met.

You cannot demand or grab love or respect. Demanding it will result only in resentment, fear, or dislike—even hatred. Grabbing it will not satiate your innermost desires for loving connections, given openly and without reservation. And that which you grab or demand will not have the mirror on the wall reflect back what you need to see.

You don't deserve anything you haven't earned. And a lot of what you get that is challenging, unpleasant, or horrific wasn't earned either. The key to a satisfying life is to strive toward the former, and survive the latter with your humanity intact. That, my friends, is not easy.

John, another listener, wrote,

"Long ago I discovered that life is a day-to-day process. Life has its BMW (Bitch, Moan, and Whine) days, and its days of joy. The bumper sticker 'S**t Happens' is a reflection of reality. One of God's little jokes is that you don't get pretty flowers without feeding them the proper amount of excrement, not too much and not too little.

"I found that the quality of my life very much depends on what I focus on and the environment that I choose. It is difficult to be negative when you make the choice to be around positive people.

"The key is choice. Are there days of profound depression? In my life, yes. Then I hear one of my trainers shout GOYA—Get Off Your 'Anatomy'—and do something about it. Sometimes doing something about it takes support, and sometimes I can do it on my own."

Open up the newspaper or turn on your computer any day and you will find page after page and blog after blog about death, mayhem, murder, betrayal, vicious reputation and personal attacks, lies, dirty politics, injustice, Hollywood stars undermining our government, ethnic cleansings, assassinations of the innocent, daily rapes and murders of mothers and children, hurricanes, tornadoes, and earthquakes claiming lives in an instant, dictators fomenting terror, and the like. It makes one wonder, "What is there to be happy about?"

Patricia submitted her answer to my radio program,

"My mother- and father-in-law taught me that life is for the living and we should never whine about how bad we had it or have it. They lived through the Depression and my mother-in-law had three bouts of cancer (breast, vaginal, colon) and is still alive and cancer free but in a nursing home with macular degeneration, osteoporosis,

and angina. But every time we visit, she asks about our day, what's new? how is the weather? . . . never complains about anything. She is eighty-eight and still conquering.

"My father-in-law died two years ago with Alzheimer's. Until the end, even when he could hardly swallow, he kept trying to help. If you came to visit, he put his drink up and pushed it toward you, offering you a drink—still in some small way trying to be of use.

"He was eighty-six when he died peacefully with his son and myself by his side. His funeral was the best attended I've ever seen, with people talking about how he always helped them and total strangers who were in need. God bless."

When I first read Patricia's letter, I choked up. Quite frankly, it is truly difficult to imagine being the slightest bit easy to get along with, cheerful about anything, caring about anyone, when you're suffering so very much. When I'm confronted on my radio show by a caller who is clearly going through a nonvoluntary hell, asking me why he or she should even bother with anyone or anything, I fall back onto two flowers from the cesspool of the Holocaust: the Righteous Gentiles (Christians who risked their lives, and those of their children and relatives, to save Jews from the Nazi death camps) and the known acts of compassion by concentration camp victims who shared their last scrap of food with someone who was soon to die anyway, or who tried to observe their religious rituals in an environment which would seem to deny the Divine.

You would think that in these circumstances, personal survival would be paramount. And of course it is . . . but not to the exclusion of what makes that survival meaningful: one's humanity and compassion for others—which ultimately precludes anyone from being a stranger.

Our country is putting the lives of American military personnel at risk to liberate people from tyranny in the hope of building democracies that respect their neighbors and the value of life—ultimately protecting Americans. Our police and firefighters put their lives on the line every day to protect the innocent. There are no strangers, just opportunities for blessings—blessings, though, which come at a price.

Sometimes that price is quite difficult to handle. Most of the time, though, people underestimate their ability to face pain. You can't watch five minutes of television without seeing an ad for some medication for the quick eradication of pain, physical or emotional. A profound clinical depression may be medical, but sadness, fear, disappointment, embarrassment, loss, frustration, etc., are just a part of normal life, and need to be endured as a feeling, and approached with solutions, if possible.

Rebecca commented on this issue:

"You took a call from a twenty-three-year-old struggling with life's relatively minor disappointments and was using antidepressants to cope. You asked her how she was going to deal with REALLY hard things. You also commented on how her generation has grown up thinking sadness is a disease. I wanted to tell you I fully agree with your opinion on this.

"On July 10, 2007, I went in for a routine prenatal appointment. I was ten weeks pregnant. I went by myself and my husband was at home watching our two girls. It was at this appointment I learned my baby had died. My baby died at nine weeks, three days, on July 4th.

"I have seared on my brain the picture of my baby perfectly still with no heartbeat. When I close my eyes it's all I can see. On July 13th I had a D&C because my body failed to miscarry my baby.

This has sent me into a tailspin. On July 21st, I went in for a 1-week checkup to see how I was doing. They asked me how I was doing emotionally and I told my doctor, 'Horribly.' She then said, 'You know, it's very common for women to have to go on antidepressants temporarily to cope with this loss.' I have thought a lot about this comment. I came home and told my husband what she said and he responded with, 'You know, that's the problem with our society. Everyone wants a quick fix and everyone wants you to be over it quickly. Don't they understand that it takes time to heal and you have to mourn?'

"I have a friend whose adult daughter died in a car accident. Her doctor immediately put her on antidepressants. I actually met her about two months after her daughter died and thought she seemed too well composed for the magnitude of the loss. About a year later she demanded to be taken off the antidepressants. You know what? She finally grieved her daughter's death. All the medication did was delay her grief.

"You are right, Dr. Laura, we have to feel ALL the feelings, not just the good ones. When someone dies or we lose them for some other reason, we grieve, and in the end that process makes us stronger.

"As for me, I am thankful for the two girls I have been given. I don't understand yet why God took my littlest angel and I will probably always wonder. Right now I cry at night so my children won't have to watch me. I haven't gone a night without crying. But I honestly would not want it any other way. My emotions and my tears validate that my baby was a person."

Most people, with time and support, survive all sorts of outrageous fortune. For those who ultimately can't, medical and psychological treatments may be helpful. I believe, though, that we should raise our children, as we did in the past, with stories of strangers and notables overcoming adversity as motivation and role models. My aunt Lucia, whom I've never met, is mine. My aunt and mother were very young women during World War II in fascist Italy under Mussolini. The Nazi SS were all over northern Italy, specifically Gorizia, their hometown. My aunt Lucia joined the underground to fight with the Allies. Unfortunately, that rebel cell had been discovered by the SS, and the day Lucia joined, she was caught, lined up with the others against a wall, and shot down.

I heard this story when I was a very little girl. At the time I heard it, it had little meaning for me outside of an interesting story about my mom's past. As I grew up and experienced more and more confusion and pain in life, the story would come back to me time and again as if to hold my head above the water. "I come from sterner stuff," I'd remind myself, "than to cave in under this." I'd think of my aunt's willingness to put her life on the line to go up against murderous fascists and Nazis, and I'd be humbled and energized.

Lisa's story brings up the issue of endurance,

"My dad was in WWII and Korea. My mom was in the British army for three years. My mom's brother was a fireman who was killed in the bombings. I think one of the greatest things I learned from my parents is you do what you have to do when you have to do it. My mom lived with bombs going off all around her and my dad had to, among other things, bring home the dead soldiers to their families.

"They didn't have time to collapse and think about how distraught

they were. Things had to be done and they did them. They didn't spend years on the psych's couch (I'm NOT knocking people who NEED therapy). They just did what they had to do. Great life lesson for me. They were truly the greatest generation."

Not everyone comes from a family with spirited and inspiring stories. Some of you grew up surrounded by perpetual sadness, anger, bitterness, and negativity even about the "good stuff." Of course that will make it difficult for you to do other than what you've been indoctrinated into; difficult does not mean impossible. First you must have the awareness that embracing suffering is a learned response, a habit.

Vani came to that awareness, and it freed her to actually experience happiness without guilt or fear:

"Once I realized I wanted to just BE HAPPY instead of continuing the family pattern I had grown up with, I decided to shut up, DO the right things, and focus on the blessings in my life instead of what was wrong. I believe happiness is a habit—not a circumstance.

"The two main things that have helped me make this transition in my life is my faith in God and my fight to always keep a positive attitude no matter what. I have to repeat myself: HAPPINESS IS A HABIT."

Let me express Vani's point in another way. You know those inkblot pictures? Well, you can focus on the dark, or you can focus on the light. Whichever you focus on will give you a different picture. You never stop being aware of the dark—in fact you check it out quite carefully. But ultimately you have the choice of which to use to discern the picture to report. Even if the light and the dark are distributed fifty-fifty you still get to choose. Even if the dark overwhelms the light you still get to choose.

You've all seen movie scenes with the death of somebody absolutely beloved. Everybody is crying and suffering. One person says, "Well, at least (s)he is no longer suffering, and we all have largely wonderful memories of a loving relationship that we can share with each other for the rest of our lives." Generally, hugs ensue, complete with tearful grins. The dark is still there, but illuminated by the light it doesn't seem quite as dark as a moment ago.

There is hardly an experience in life that doesn't have a dark side. It becomes a daily struggle to fight against the mesmerizing pull of the dark, and when the dark side keeps its edge, you lose appreciating the texture and joy of living.

Another listener wrote,

"You can only sit there for so long and whine and whine. It gets so tiring on both sides to make everything so dramatic all the time. Who has the time or energy? Life is too short for all the drama."

I take a lot of time in my book *Bad Childhood—Good Life* explaining how sadness and hurt can trap us into a mind-set of hopelessness. Suffice it to say, we all want to feel good, but we don't all know how to do that when we're suffering. And sometimes the suffering becomes our way of life and relating to others, in the hope that their ministering to us will erase the facts that pain us. It doesn't work and we get trapped.

I talk every day to innumerable people caught in this web; they want to feel good, but giving up the suffering becomes frightening, as it has been their reality for so long. They'll struggle against my recommendations and lament that others seem to be abandoning them, tired of the whining, which, instead of being a signal for change, merely becomes another reason for sadness.

Convincing people from this background that it is actually possible to be happy, in spite of real problems—past and present— is quite a challenge. It is a beautiful thing to see someone move from a vantage point of complaining about circumstances to making that lemonade:

"I will be a stay-at-home mom in thirty days," writes Linda, a listener.

"Honestly, I couldn't do this until I stopped the whining, rehashing, complaining, suffering about being a mother and realized it was a blessing and something I wanted to do full-time.

"How did I get here? First, I stopped hanging around women who were SAHMs and miserable and complaining.

"Second, I fought off the last remnants of my feminist days that told me that my husband could and would leave me and I had to be strong enough and ready to take care of myself. He deserved for me to have faith in him as he never showed me otherwise.

"Lastly, I slowed down time and took my focus off having a perfectly clean house. My focus is now 100 percent on my husband and kids. Supportive, positive friends are the only ones I have any of my precious time to share with."

What put Linda in perspective of the "light" was a realization that she was stopping herself from enjoying the very thing she wanted to do—largely because of peer pressure and "feminista" negativity about femininity, motherhood, and homemaker. This took immense courage, since the defensive response of her old friends was probably ostracism and attacks.

Some people don't come to this awareness all by themselves;

they have to be pushed by a real friend. Many callers profess being a good or even best friend to someone they are not truthful with at all. They are actually more concerned with losing the friendship than being a true friend: someone who will risk the loss of the relationship to help the other move from the dark to the light side.

Fortunately, Candace had a good friend, and trusted her enough to listen and learn:

"My best friend since childhood said (when I was twenty), 'You say you hate how your mom complains and is so critical yet you are just like her!' Talk about a stab thru the gut! It made me think of Proverbs 27:6, 'Faithful are the wounds of a friend, but deceitful are the kisses of an enemy.'

"I knew she was right—after the shock of hearing that and having to come face-to-face with the truth, but it was a turning point in my life.

"I designated a year to concentrate on thanking God for EVERYTHING big and small. It didn't matter if it was a particularly beautiful dandelion growing thru a crack in a city sidewalk—I forced myself to pray and thank the Lord for that weed. It proved a pivotal decision and completely changed my life.

"People have told me they wished they could be as positive and happy as I am. My cup is truly half full. I try to continue to always thank God for the small stuff as I now raise my three daughters with the constant message, 'Nothing is a problem, it's only an opportunity.'"

Some of you reading Candace's "cup half full" perspective probably think that this sort of Pollyanna-like thinking isn't real, possible, or sustaining. Well, you're right. At any given moment even Candace can slip into despair, but her experience with gratitude to God gives her somewhere to go before her pain causes her to set down roots on the dark side.

No matter what you've suffered or continue to suffer, while you are alive you have the opportunity to get something from this life —and I'm going to do my best to help you with that.

I believe I am very qualified to help you do this, as I am a trained, experienced, licensed psychotherapist (Marriage and Family Therapy) with more than thirty years of helping people, first in private practice, and now mostly through my daily radio program; but even more, I know of what I speak, as this has been my torturous journey also. I came from a family of much negativity and unhappiness, and it has been a difficult transition from being angry and scared a lot of the time, having to be perfect or punished, and fearing that all disappointments and failures were terminal, to being freed up enough to admit that to you, dear reader!

Cassie once e-mailed me with her quote of the day on http://en.thinkexist.com, a quotations database: "'*The people and circumstances around me do not make me what I am, they reveal who I am.*' That quote is from Dr. Laura Schlessinger." While I was most pleased to see myself quoted, I kept this as a reminder to myself. Hopefully this book will be that for you.

Blessings,

Dr. Laura Schlessinger

CHAPTER 1

Perspective Is Everything

"I have changed my life from 'talking, whining, rehashing, complaining, and suffering' into a life of doing and enduring because I got tired. I got tired of MAKING THE CHOICE to have a bad attitude. I realized almost at the 'ripe' old age of thirty that I alone am responsible for my behaviors and my moods; and whining and the rest of that nonsense is futile to resolution and problem solving.

"I suppose the main catalyst for this life change was putting things in PERSPECTIVE; I haven't had a charmed life but I also realize how BLESSED I have been. I think all those people who claim that they are unhappy are only that way because they do not know how to appreciate what they DO have. It is hard not to take for granted what one has, but at the same time it is hard to believe that most people who have so much are still so miserable."

—WENDY, A LISTENER

I talk a lot about perspective on my radio program to callers who just can't seem to break the hold that emotional pain, disappointments, and fears have on them. I'm usually met first with their annoyance, as though I'm trying to strip them of what is most important in their lives—their suffering and their anger about it. As anyone who has ever dealt with children knows, if you grab something out of the hand of a cranky kid, you'd better be ready to put something else in its place. Well, with callers on the phone, what I have to put back in their minds after grabbing their complaints (justified or not—it doesn't matter) is a more compelling image.

That substitute image has to:

1. Make sense to them

2. Not ignore or deny their suffering or the reasons for it

3. Touch them more deeply than the reason they have for suffering

4. Motivate behavior in a new and healthier direction

5. Provide a direction for action

6. Overpower resistance now and the likelihood of falling back into old patterns in the future

Let me move straightaway to some examples of how this works in real life. One recent caller in particular sticks in my mind for this demonstration, as the call was powerful with a very quick turnabout in attitude and perspective.

A young woman, about twenty-three, called concerning her sexual orientation and whether or not she should tell her mother. She was afraid that her mother would not be approving.

The very first thing I told her was "I'll bet your mother knows. She can't have lived with you for over two decades and not have an inkling. . . . She is a mother! It is not unusual, however, for parents to seemingly ignore situations like this because of their fears and feelings."

The next thing I told her was "You have to understand that this is foreign to your mother, who has loved a man all her adult life, and who, as a loving mother, worries about what you'll be missing out on that she has cherished for a lifetime. She may never approve of (embrace) your orientation, but given a chance, she'll probably be lovingly accepting (tolerant)."

It was at this point that I worked more directly on perspective: "It isn't all about you, although I realize you see it that way. Your mother loses one of her dreams—her daughter's wedding and marriage to a son-in-law and eventual grandchildren, and without that, she doesn't see a clear role for herself in your future. Your mother will suffer for her losses as well as her concerns about yours. I think you need to be less prickly and worried, and more compassionate."

The caller's attitude changed abruptly from fearful and whiny to hopeful and concerned. Her mission became one of mutuality instead of one that was totally defensive. She hung up feeling more understanding of the bigger picture, of which she was but one part. Pictures must be seen from a multitude of vantage points to be seen clearly and properly appreciated.

The Everyday

I wish I had a dollar for every woman who called complaining about her husband not doing enough housework. Such women usually first tell me what a great guy he is in general, and then they get to their specific complaint concerning his sloppiness. Most advice show hosts generally go into strategies to manipulate, threaten, demand, or negotiate him into housework. I work on perspective.

Traci, a listener, wrote:

"You've talked before about keeping things in perspective and I just felt the need to reiterate the point. My husband, who is my hero, my swimmer of shark-infested waters, the sole financial supporter of our family of four, and the wonderful father to my two small girls, can absolutely annoy the CRAP out of me sometimes!!! He can take the can opener out of the drawer, place it on the counter right above,

and never put it back; his dirty clothes are typically on the floor somewhere near the dirty clothes hamper. He thinks everything that is in the garage NEEDS to be put back in its proper place however those things that belong in the house are of less importance. I could go on . . .

"But then on occasion, I manage to remember who he is; he is a public servant. It is what he was born to do. He protects people. He is a state trooper, a volunteer firefighter, and an officer in the Coast Guard Reserves (after five years active duty Air Force and two years Air Force Reserves).

"He is a man who, except for the occasional fishing trip, spends his spare time at home with his family. So I face the reality nearly every single time he walks out that door . . . he might not come back. You know what? When I remember to put it in that light, it really doesn't matter where the can opener or his socks end up. I would much rather spend every day of the rest of my life taking care of such items behind him, than live a moment of my life without him.

"Perhaps together, Dr. Laura, we can remind wives out there that having a wonderful husband that doesn't care so much that things are always in their proper place is a far cry better than having no wonderful husband at all!"

Once I read that e-mail on my radio program, other women wrote in with similar stories. Julie, another listener, wrote that she used to complain all the time to her family about her husband's lack of neatness in their home. That continued until November 2005, when her best friend lost her husband.

Julie related that the husband was a wonderful man and her friend and he had a mutually adoring relationship. She remembered that her friend never complained about him at all! In November 2005 he died in the line of duty as a highway patrol officer. After Julie watched her friend grieve, it dawned on her that she would never have an opportunity to complain about him, ever. That changed her attitude toward her whole family, especially her husband. She realized her friend would give up anything just to have to pick up after her husband.

Julie had written to me right after hearing me talk to a wife complaining about the disorder in her home due to the lack of her husband's help. I had reminded the caller that there is evidence of "life" in her home, since things are moved around, not picked up, and not organized. Julie responded,

"That hit home for me! The hardest part of living alone again, my friend says, is nothing changes unless she changes it. She leaves the house and things are still the same when she comes back. She goes days without having to 'clean' because she picks up after herself as she goes. But I see the longing for her to have someone to pick up after. I often let her wash our dishes after we share a meal, not only because I hate washing dishes, but because it gives her a sense of belonging and purpose. So—moral of the story—pitch your socks off and hug your hubby."

Leanne, the proud wife of a deployed marine, also responded to that call:

"I was pushed over the edge when the caller said that her husband was home more than others, but that meant that he made more of a mess. I also have small children, two and a half and seven months. I would gladly pick up socks and put down the toilet seat all day long just to have the companionship and comfort of my spouse; and I would put away any dish left anywhere in the home if it meant

*that my son didn't have to ask me again when Daddy would be
home from war—knowing that I can't give him the answer that he
wants."*

Close your eyes—well, after reading this paragraph through
first—and picture the person in your life who is causing you
annoyance (note: annoyance is not about a dangerous or destructive
spouse). First picture all those things the person does that irritate
you no end! Really work on that—get yourself riled up!

Then pluck the person out of the picture of your world and see
what would change, what you would lose and miss. If you had to
and could choose, which picture would you want to keep?

Real life requires a sense of humor and a margin of forgiveness.
The sense of humor helps you accept the things you cannot change
by transforming them into smiles, and forgiveness helps you let go
of the bitterness that gets in the way of loving life. Some quirks,
weaknesses, and dumb habits are just not worth getting worked
up over. Everybody's got 'em, including you!

It comes down to this: do you really think you'll be happy only
when everything and everyone around you is and does things
exactly the way you wish? Then, my friends, you'll never be
happy; and neither will anybody be happy with you!

Hardship: A Matter of Pride or Pain?

When we are suffering over something, our world collapses
in to contain only ourselves; we become like a vegetable covered
with heated shrink-wrap. It is really tough to fight out of that

shrink-wrap because the suffering sucks us into that vortex of self-centeredness.

John wrote about how he worked out of that miserable state of mind:

"What turned my approach to life around, from victim to true adulthood, was a hard look at how tough life was for those who have gone before me. It was not that long ago that life expectancy was significantly lower than it is today, and life was often filled with illness, oppression, and heartache.

"During what I considered to be a 'hard day,' I strolled along the Illinois and Michigan Canal during lunch, considering the brutal conditions through which those who dug the canal labored.

"Disease, injury, exposure to the elements, loneliness, and backbreaking work endured for a pittance—and they worked well in excess of my 'marathon' eight-hour day.

"In their limited spare time, they built churches up and down the canal, some of which still stand today, along with their tombstones.

"Whenever my 'poor me' attitude surfaces, I think of what my ancestors endured, awed by their grit, perseverance, and faith."

Hardship is simply a fact of life, not a personal assault on you, and while you may have it bad—so do others. What does that mean for you? Are you not entitled to express pain, hurt, or anger simply because others are suffering too? Of course you're entitled to your pain. Now what?

A talk-show host on a Los Angeles station has one response to those who come on the air with him by asking how he's doing: "Better than some and not as good as others." The first time I heard him say that I thought it was very cute. After that I thought, "How profound." And what a good message.

Anne wrote about taking her two-year-old son out to lunch. She was feeling frustrated that day because her husband has to travel several times a month for work and because her son is in the terrible twos. She thought she'd take a break and go out for a bite. She ended up sitting next to a woman who had two children with her.

The woman mentioned that she had two children in school and the ones with her were five and one. Immediately Anne felt foolish for feeling overwhelmed with one kidlet. Anne said, "You have your hands full!" The woman said, "Yep . . . and my husband is in Iraq." She went on to explain that the youngest son has a kidney disease and is on a transplant list.

Anne continued,

"It hit me like a brick. I have a husband who works terribly hard to take care of me and our son. Both my son and husband are healthy. I was also aware that because of her husband's sacrifice for our country she was raising her four children on about half the salary that my husband earns each year.

"It occurred to me that whining about my small problems is self-serving and useless. Now when it occurs to me to feel sorry for myself, I think about this woman—her sacrifice, her husband's sacrifice, and how lucky we are as a family.

"Life is about gratitude. Even on my toughest days, I have precious little to complain about."

Of course there are things worthy of complaining about or being upset over. However, the depth, breadth, and duration of your emotional reaction—and the drain on your well-being and ability to enjoy the other aspects of your life—can be lessened with perspective.

Sally came to this understanding the hard way:

"I won first prize in the 'poor me' contest. I loved the blame game and laying guilt.

"What changed that was my husband's triple bypass. It wasn't all about me anymore. Then, to strengthen my transition, was my own battle with breast cancer.

"When faced with death, all matters become small in comparison. I actually found my sense of humor again and compassion for others. I also found great pleasure in helping others.

"My husband and I were brought to our knees when we learned he not only needed another bypass (at sixty) but had a rapidly growing aortic aneurysm that could burst at any time. Even those who are not believers become so with that kind of news.

"Both surgeries were successful and we live our lives now with immense gratitude and deep love."

I bet that most of you are wondering how it is at all possible for anyone to have a positive perspective when facing possible imminent or painful death. Imagine for a moment that you've been thrown into raging waters. At first you flail about and scream like crazy; you're full of fear and confusion. Then you have two options: one is to continue the frenzied behavior; the other is to look for something or someone to hold on to, be it some floating debris, a Coast Guard rescuer, your swimming skills, God through prayer, or lovely memories.

It is said that just before you die your whole life flashes before your eyes. If that is so, I'll bet it is never the ugly memories; it is typically those lovely moments that make life memorable and worth living.

This type of transition in thought and emotion does not happen automatically. Believe me, sometimes you really have to make an effort to force yourself into it. I can confirm that firsthand. It is much easier to stay with the enraged defense against whatever assault has occurred than raise your gaze toward the sky and feel gratitude for being alive; that fact gives you options for a better tomorrow.

"Oh Yeah, That's True, Isn't It?"

Elephants may remember everything, but human beings seem to readily forget some of the most important truths and realities of their lives. That forgetfulness is usually called "taking someone/something for granted." That which doesn't cause us fear·or pain seems to have the longevity of a wisp of smoke. It's a shame. We all need reminding.

Katie, mother of two little boys, called me recently about her compulsive overeating and overspending.

Dr. Laura: So you've made yourself fat and poor?

Katie: Fortunately I decided to take up running last year to keep the fat at bay, but I'm getting close to being poor, and you know this staying-at-home part is very important to me. I'm putting that in jeopardy by doing the things that I do.

Katie mostly spends her money on clothes. She brings them home and sticks them somewhere, anywhere. Then, as time wears on, she ends up getting rid of them and getting new ones and the cycle continues.

Dr. Laura: Tell me the feeling that happens just before you feel the need to go shopping.

Katie: Y'know . . .

Dr. Laura: No, no, no. Don't talk until you know what the feeling is. Shhh. Don't talk. All I want to know is the one or two words to the feeling.

Katie: (voice breaking) Emptiness.

Dr. Laura: Emptiness. Okay. That made you cry.

Katie: I know.

Dr. Laura: And when was the first time you remember having the feeling of emptiness?

Katie: Probably a great while ago.

Katie then talked about her parents' divorce. She said that she really did think that the divorce was a good thing because of all the continual family upheaval that preceded it. I told her that regardless of how she felt about her parents' divorce, it was still devastating to her. As crappy as they might have been together, it was still family.

Katie: Yeah. (long sigh)

Dr. Laura: You're still sad.

Katie: Yeah, I am. I've been depressed.

I pointed out to Katie that she isn't depressed when she's running; she's not depressed when she's buying either, nor when having a yummy dessert. She's depressed only when she's alone with her thoughts, which seem to behave like homing pigeons and go right back to her original family's demise.

Dr. Laura: Well, you know what? Here's the good news: if you truly had a profound clinical depression, you'd be depressed through all of that. The bad news is this: you forget—now listen to me very, very carefully—you forget that you're not empty anymore. You were when your parents imploded. What happens to you that you call depression, is that you tap into the emptiness of the first half of your life, and then you forget that you're not empty anymore.

Katie: That's right!

Dr. Laura: And, gosh darn, there are people who like you, who admire you. There are two kids who look up to you as the transitional object between them and God. You gave them life. Your husband looks at you with awe because you're the mother of his children, and his woman, for whom he slays dragons.

Your life is very full, but it's like a train track switch . . . you sometimes switch into yesterday and switch out of today. Wrong track.

There's nothing empty about you now. Just switch that track over. Actually visualize the train track. When it goes by the next time (when you start getting that empty feeling), actually see the train track and switch it over. And then enjoy the beautiful view you have on the "all filled up" track!

Look at any garden: among the lovely colorful blooms and aroma is dirt filled with dog poop, crawly bugs, dead leaves, and petals. Before the flowers germinated and then bloomed, there was only the dirt. But now you have lovely flowers and you can choose to focus on the flowers or the crud. That there always will be some dirt and crawly bugs and such between the flowers is a fact of life. Somehow, though, the contrast between the bugs and the blooms makes the blooms even more special.

My Body, Myself

An area of sensitivity to just about every woman who has ever lived is her looks. I've had way too many women call me about not having sex with their husbands because they are embarrassed that they have gained or lost weight; that they have C-section scars, skin saggy with age; and so forth. In addition, the women behave like jealous harpies whenever they're around other women or even watching actresses on television or movies. This constant self-disgust gets in the way of enjoying their lives.

Sometimes the cause of the "imperfection" is quite serious; however, the concept of "perception" is still everything.

Jackie called to announce she had stage 2 breast cancer. Her mammogram had been clear, but she had what felt like a painful cyst in her breast. After a biopsy, she was diagnosed with cancer and was having a double mastectomy—the second breast being removed to minimize the possibility of a recurrence. She was scheduled to have reconstructive surgery.

Jackie had been married for nineteen years to a sergeant with the L.A. County Sheriff's Department, who took time off to sit with her during her chemo. A very good guy.

Jackie: Which kind of brings me to my question. I mean, this has been an incredible experience for us to go through together. He's been amazing. Of course, he's told me that he thinks I'm beautiful no matter what I look like.

Dr. Laura: Yeah, and you don't believe that.

Jackie: I believe that he thinks that (laughs), but, y'know, as a woman, part of feeling sexy is feeling sexy yourself.

Dr. Laura: Yes, but, Jackie, with two breasts, you didn't have the best body in the world anyway!

Jackie: (laughing) You know me!!

Dr. Laura: Well, yeah, because none of us has the best body in the world. Close your eyes. Now I want you to feel the moment when you and your husband are making love, and he's running his hand over your body. That feels great, doesn't it?

Jackie: Umm-hmm.

Dr. Laura: Even though if you open your eyes and look at your body, it's not the best body in the world?

Jackie: Right.

The truth is that if every woman made love to her husband only when she thought she was a hot babe, there'd be nobody out there doing it because we women are all neurotic about our bodies.

Jackie's husband had been with her for nearly two decades. He loves her. I'm sure he would prefer her to have two breasts—guys like breasts! But because he knew she had cancer, he was scared to lose her.

Dr. Laura: Jackie, if he had only one testicle would you stop making love to him?

Jackie: No—because I love HIM.

Dr. Laura: When he's rubbing his hands over the length of your body when you two are making love, it feels very good to his hand, even if what's under his hand isn't perfect. That's because he's touching the woman he adores, and if he could lay his hand on your chest where your boob is no more, and make it all better, he'd give his hand!

Jackie: I know.

Dr. Laura: Don't stop making love, because you are *making love*, which is different from just having sex. See, a lot of people are just having sex—in which case the guy probably won't want to touch an imperfect chest. Your husband makes love to you—so for him nothing has changed. He still wants to touch the body of his woman and you still want to be touched.

So for the first few times, you'll probably feel kind of awkward and stupid—he will too. And then . . . you won't . . . because it'll all feel so good again.

This perspective also holds for everyday, non-life-threatening body image issues. Nobody gets to middle age and on without some dimpling, wrinkling, sagging, and bagging—it's an inevitable part of life. Too many women, like a recent caller, Andrea, struggle "a lot with comparing myself to every single woman I see."

Dr. Laura: You mean for looks?

Andrea: Yeah, it's all about looks.

Dr. Laura: Oh. Okay. You're prettier than some; uglier than others. That is true for me, you, and for every other woman on the face of the earth.

While that made rational sense to Andrea, the point was that she was completely obsessed with making these comparisons: judging other women and measuring her worth by how she measures up.

Andrea: Everywhere I am, everywhere I go with my husband—especially if he's there—I feel like I am a complete, disgusting loser. . . .

Dr. Laura: A loser is about action—not about looks.

Andrea: What I'm saying is that I've developed this thinking that men are just lustful pigs.

Dr. Laura: Actually you're correct . . . until they're married . . . and then they lust for the woman who brings them the security and warmth, who is the mother of their children, the woman who makes them feel accepted, who makes them feel masculine. Any babe walking down the street can't do that—she can only arouse the "animal" instinct. So when men get married, it all morphs into a dependency on how their woman treats them, not as much on how she looks anymore.

Andrea: Wow! Okay.

Dr. Laura: Maybe if your husband met you now for the first time, he'd look at your body, which, y'know, has a little more cellulite, and is a little more saggy here and there, and it wouldn't be the *first* thing that turned him on. But you *do* turn him on—because of what you *are* to him.

Andrea: That's what he says!

Dr. Laura: He's telling you the truth.

Andrea: I get carried away in wanting to be his every desire. I want to be the one who will make his head turn when he walks down the street and sees me.

Dr. Laura: Honey, honey, honey. When you're ninety-five, are you still going to talk like this? He's not superficial. He notices beauty in others, but lives for the beauty you give him. You are neglecting him, his soul, his being, if the only thing you think of giving him is your looks. He needs more than that.
Andrea: Oh yeah, you're so right.

The problem with so many issues of suffering and unhappiness is that we look at only one sliver of the situation—and from that view, of course it looks grim! But when we stand back and approach the problem as though we're looking through a wide-angle lens, there are so many other aspects of the issue.

If, like Andrea's, your personal value and power of attraction with a man have been largely an issue of beauty, then aging and competing with others via comparisons become painful. As I tried—and I believe managed—to have Andrea understand, her value to her husband was so much more than her looks, which were only one small and not even the most important quality to her man. With this perspective, hopefully she began to see herself through her meaning to him, fulfilled by her *actions* of appreciation, admiration, affection, respect, and compassion.

The issue of perspective here has to do with the difference between how we narrowly see the world, and what we *really mean* in that world.

Your Pain Ricochets

Jennifer called my radio program to complain about her manipulative and abusive father. She described herself as weak when it came to him. Whenever she had anything to talk to him about she felt like a fifteen-year-old girl asking his permission to do something. She recognized that since this bothered her so much, it impacted her relationship with her husband not only through her mood swings, but by her taking it out on him.

Dr. Laura: You've become abusive.

Jennifer: I have? What do you mean?

Dr. Laura: Well, you've permitted yourself to get into a perpetual state in which you cause your husband pain, hurt, frustration, maybe even anger.

Jennifer: Well, yes, that is true.

Dr. Laura: That's abusive. If being with your father creates such a state in you that you turn around and abuse your husband, then you have to make a choice, because it looks like you can't handle both. You have to make a choice if you're gonna be the little girl still trying to get Daddy's approval, or a grown woman having a healthy, loving marriage.

When you don't get what you want from your dad, your husband gets the brunt of it.

Jennifer: You're absolutely right.

Dr. Laura: Is that any different than your father when he doesn't get what he wants?

Jennifer: (silence)

Dr. Laura: He takes it out on his children.

Jennifer: Yeah. (quietly)

Dr. Laura: Then what's the difference?

Jennifer: None. I love my husband and my children more than anything—so they come first in my life.

Dr. Laura: Then you have to say it to yourself in your head, "I have to give up trying to make my father love me." Let me hear you say that, Jennifer.

Jennifer: I have to give up making my father love me.

Dr. Laura: And tell me something, Jennifer, isn't sitting there being the good little girl, isn't that manipulative?

Jennifer: Yes, actually it is. 'Cause I'm not being myself.

Dr. Laura: Well, the whole way you described your dad, you described yourself.

Jennifer: I never really looked at it like that before. Well, I really respect your opinion—and that's helped me out a lot.

And there it is: a quick change from suffering, frustration, and confusion to being committed and focused, as well as relieved. You wouldn't think that pointing out to a person that she is doing something "bad" would ultimately result in a feeling of joy, would you? Well, this shift in perspective works best with only the most decent of people: people who are caring and concerned about their impact on others. In this case, it was just that in her long-term and frustrating search for parental validation (the blood-from-a-stone version), she lost sight of what validation she received in the here and now.

For some people it is as though they can't go on to enjoy today and tomorrow without the permission from yesterday. When that permission is unavailable, they feel stuck and confused—and unworthy.

I try to remind these callers that unless they see their current spouses, children, friends, etc., as completely stupid, somebody obviously sees them as more than worthy; however, they jeopardize that by insisting that yesterday catch up.

Let it go.

Mirror, Mirror on the Wall . . .

Sometimes the simplest change in perspective has to do with how you see yourself. If you see yourself as "crippled," then, of course, you'll "limp." If you see yourself as "healthy and strong," then you'll strut your stuff.

Lisa had been raised in a strife-ridden household. As a child she coped with great difficulties and suffered from chronic headaches, constipation, insomnia, obesity, depression, and general angst. The constant second-guessing of herself wore her out. Large chunks of time were spent with her musing over what she should have done, how she could have done better, and so forth.

"At twenty-one, after much soul-searching and years of prayer, I had an inspiration. One day, while grocery shopping, a thought from heaven occurred to me: What if I'm not a defective person? What if I'm normal and this is just life? This thought opened up my life and altered the way I viewed myself. From that point forward I came to accept that I was not starkly different from other people, but shared in a common human drama.

"While not a miraculous cure, that was a starting point for a reframing of my thinking. Gradually the health problems disappeared and I became capable of joy and chose to associate with faithful and hope-filled people. New life!"

Yes, indeed, just join the human race; better than some, not as good as others, but always striving for the heavens—AND—with an attitude of loving appreciation for the opportunities, not a self-loathing discounting of your potential.

Closing Sentiment

This contribution is from Patricia:

"It is not easy having post-polio syndrome, diabetes and a heart condition, an adult son with autism, and being estranged from my youngest. My middle child is my rock. We have fun together. I never worry about what I can't do, because there are so many things I can do that bring me joy. How can one not smile when you can look at the beautiful sunrise and sunset. So, see? I do not have a problem."

Hopefully, we will all learn to *see*.

CHAPTER 2

Talk! Talk? Talk! Talk?

"I have learned that there is great power in taking action in directions where I have complaints or have been wronged by someone—and most of all, by taking forward steps instead of dredging up the past and displaying my suffering. I was like everyone else who complains and blames everything bad that 'happens' to me on my circumstances or parents: growing up in an abusive household with divorced parents.

"For a while, people jumped for me when I told them how 'sad' my childhood was. But there comes a point when no one cares anymore. Then God blessed me with the greatest man in the world. My husband didn't put up with the whining, just showed me how to move forward. He put me in my place, by not only telling me to quit the complaining and do something—but by leading by example."

—MARIANNE, A LISTENER

I host a daily, three-hour radio TALK show, during which time people call me to TALK about their ethical, moral, and interpersonal problems. So what is it? Are you supposed to talk about your emotional problems or not? Does it help or hurt?

The answer is actually simple: at first it can help; later, it probably hurts more than it helps.

I recently had a caller whose whiny voice when she came on the air immediately told me volumes about her general demeanor and behavior. While she was sadly stumbling around in her attempts to ultimately ask me a question, she kept bouncing around her past with her complaints.

I asked her, "Do you have a problem *today*?" As she kept trying to tell me yet another ancient story, I kept repeating, "Do you have a problem *today*?" My memory is that I interrupted her about five or six times with that question until she finally said, "Well, no, but . . ."

She was married, with two small children. I asked her if she had a nice husband. Affirmative. I asked her if her children were healthy and adorable. Affirmative. I asked her why she would want to bring her admittedly ugly past into her lovely present with such determination? She got quiet, but only for an instant. And it started all over again, the whining about what she doesn't get—what she never got—from her family.

"I thought you just told me that your husband and children were blessings?"

I was trying to get her to differentiate past from present, original family from current family, what was in her control—enjoying the present—and not in her control—rewriting her past. At least during this phone call, I failed to accomplish that. I can only hope that she thought about it more later and came to realize that retroactive suffering is ultimately useless and destructive.

Discussing problems as a means of finding a deeper understanding or solution is exceptionally healthy. Perpetual rumination is only destructive. Overtalking about problems enforces the focus on the negative aspects of the problem(s) and deepens feelings of anxiety, depression, and hopelessness.

In other words, there is effective complaining and ineffective complaining. Ineffective complaining has an intent other than solving the problem. Dana, a listener, wrote an e-mail which helps clarify this point:

"I have learned that I am in control of my attitude; it's a choice to keep talking, whining, rehashing, complaining, or suffering, because doing all these things is an attempt to get the attention of someone else. Furthermore, it doesn't help anything.

"Instead, talking about the problem should be [aimed at] assessing

whatever situation you are in, without all the emotions, and then seeing what next step you can do to change, fix, or adjust the situation.

"Dr. Laura, I learned this from you. Thank you, because people are seeing me taking care of business maturely and not responding to situations like a teen; moreover, I'm getting more respect.

"We are women; we need to do some of this talking and talking— it relieves stress. I limit it to only a few close friends. I give a disclaimer before I do this, telling her that I am just complaining and/or whining because I need to vent, not because I need advice or I am confused. If I am upset about something, sometimes I can only gripe and complain for only thirty minutes a day—and then that's that!"

As I clarified in chapter 1 on perspective, getting feedback and another set of eyes on a problem is a very positive, healthy thing to do. However, it requires you to actually be open to this information, and willing to run with it, away from the negativity and into a constructive transition in thought, feeling, and deed.

As Dana and Marianne have already pointed out, there is a temptation to use ruminating on hurt feelings and problems in order to get people to feel sorry for you, take care of you, cut you slack—in other words, get babied because that just feels so good.

However, as Dana pointed out, it loses you respect.

Stacey, another listener, wrote:

"Three years ago I lost my father and touchstone to a heart attack, my husband of twenty-five years to infidelity (I had my part and should have read The Proper Care and Feeding of Husbands *ten years earlier), and my youngest daughter to her first years of college all in the same month. It was a lot of prayer and listening to your advice to maligned callers that has helped me to heal and move forward with life.*

"One especially poignant call literally changed my life and moved me from a maligned victim to a woman that took control of her life. The caller was complaining that her close friend no longer seemed 'there' for her whenever she tried to talk to her about her divorce. You asked her how long ago the divorce had occurred and when she responded, 'Two years,' you said, 'Well, she's not listening to you anymore because you've become boring.' You went on to explain that people are there for you after a divorce—for which you should be grateful—but after a while the healing needs to be done in private.

"How right you are! I saw myself so clearly in that caller, that after laughing and crying at the same time, I proceeded to call my best friend and also my sister and apologized for being boring! In both instances I had good, heartfelt conversations and have been able to remain close to these two dear women."

Stacey went on in her e-mail to say that of course there are still—and always will be—times when she mourns the loss of her father and a twenty-five-year marriage and the breakup of a nuclear family, but she does so in private. She also wrote about the "uplift" aspects of this transformation: she was no longer a victim. She had chosen to move on and live a wonderful, productive life, and has met and married a terrific guy. None of which would have happened had she stayed in the mode of using each person in her life as an opportunity to garner sympathy for her valid sorrows.

Complaining as a Lifestyle

How does the joke about girlfriends go? We girls get together to shop, eat, gossip, and complain about our boyfriends/husbands!

Well, the shopping and eating make us happy immediately; gossiping gives us a momentary twinge of false superiority; complaining about our primary relationship makes us downright miserable personally, not to mention lousy mates because we are so focused on ourselves, and continue to solidify a negative feeling about someone toward whom we are supposed to be loving.

Becki, a listener, learned that the hard way:

"About six years ago all I did was complain about my miserable marriage and my jerk of a husband. It got so bad that my friends wanted little or nothing to do with me. I couldn't understand why nobody would call me back, and why they were always busy when I tried to get together.

"Finally it happened; one of them told me how unpleasant I was. I was furious! How dare they! Didn't they know I was suffering? Couldn't they just support me?

"I decided that I would stick it to them. I would never say another negative thing about my life to them again. I wouldn't share a thing—even if it killed me.

"What happened was amazing. My circumstances didn't change; my situation actually got worse for a couple of years. But because I was sticking it to my friends by refusing to whine, bitch, and complain, I had to look hard for fun and uplifting things to talk about."

Interestingly, there are always "fun and uplifting" things to talk about. What is the point of having blessings if you're going to bury them deep in order to build an altar to suffering and unhappiness? What status and ultimate satisfaction can there be in portraying yourself as oppressed, pathetically sad, and completely miserable?

While that portrayal might get you some immediate sympathy and solicitous behavior, ultimately you will lose people's interest and respect. Think about it: all the people you whine to have problems too, and they're putting those problems and their own pain aside to be caretaking of you. If you never "move on" with their loving support, they feel like frustrated failures and disconnect from you as there is no reciprocity of caretaking.

"I became a happier person," Becki continued. *"I was so impressed with myself that I decided to branch out and do things that helped and uplifted other people. My life is much better now."*

Her life is much better now. And she is in control instead of permitting herself to ignore her blessings and become a slave to her curses.

Suffering in Silence

A certain amount of suffering has to be done internally and just accepted as a normal and universal part of life. A bit o' sadness and anxiety is the price of living. This is a subject I deal with quite often on my radio program. I find myself telling more and more callers that what they are experiencing simply needs to be endured—and that there isn't necessarily a solution or pharmaceutical prescription to eradicate every human emotion and reasonable reaction to life's challenges.

In a recent interview, I was asked how I coped with my son being in combat in the Middle East. I searched around for some clever response . . . but the truth is, I just live with it. Sometimes, upon hearing the news report that some soldiers died today, I tighten up inside; other times, I grow concerned when too much time has gone by without any contact. Generally I just live with it. I do what I tell so many callers they have to do: *endure.*

I endure by not talking about it often—that just increases anxiety by focusing my thoughts on all the horrible things that could happen. I endure by keeping busy with my work: writing this book and giving advice and direction on the air that help other people. I endure by taking hikes, shooting pool, reading novels, and going sailing . . . oh yes, can't leave out shopping! I endure by helping other military families deal with their fears or their grief. I endure sometimes just by consciously shoving it out of my mind with music.

I don't forget; I endure.

If you dance with the pain you will find that it gets a stronger and stronger hold on you. Stephanie wrote about that:

"My story is an old one: pain, pain, and pain—and, of course, all my parents' fault. I spent HOURS rehashing all the awful things that had been done to me. Then one day, in the middle of an argument, my sweet, patient, brand-new husband said to me, 'It's always something with you, isn't it?'

"That remark hurt. But it wouldn't have hurt if it wasn't so true. From that day on, with the grace of God, I became a woman and left that needy, whiny, damsel-in-distress behind. It wasn't a matter of getting 'closure.' It was simply a matter of 'stopping'!

"I stopped complaining. I stopped rehashing, analyzing, and TRYING to move on, and actually DID move on. And amazingly, when I stopped whining, the pain lost its hold on my life.

"Now I am blessed with a great marriage, a delightful son, and a new baby due this fall. The ironic part is that there has been bigger

pain in the past years than I ever had during my childhood. But it no longer owns me."

There are some very profound concepts in Stephanie's letter:

1. Closure isn't necessary—or sometimes even possible. Many of you are looking for a perfect redress of past hurts (big or small), a complete turnaround of the behavior of the offending parties, or a complete cessation of memory and emotion about what occurred. As they say on *The Sopranos*, "Fuggedaboutit!"

   Most of that wish list rarely comes true. And it is very wise to let go of a persistently rotting rope, isn't it?

2. Trying to make things be different by going over them again and again only fixates you in the past. Letting go of that rotting rope with your hand firmly gripping a better philosophy, a wise counselor, or a loving friend or relative as a cheering squad gives you the possibility of greater peace and happiness.

3. "Poop" happens—continuously. If it isn't one thing, it's a tornado or moles under your lawn, illness, or a housing market decline. It's always something. If you can't be the tree that bends, you'll break.

Although this seems like feminine treason, not everything is worth talking about, not everything bad is worth perpetually rehashing and analyzing, and certainly not everything is worth whining about.

If you cannot or are not going to change "it," perhaps it is healthier and more beneficial to your well-being (and that of the other person whom you'd bug to death with it) to simply leave it be. It'll provide you with more energy to give toward the things that really matter—the things that are truly important to the quality of your life.

The "Right" Advice

Talking about your pain and problems is a potentially useful way to get solace, support, and advice at a time of confusion and overwhelming pain. It is important, though, that you not just bounce about town talking to whoever will listen—not everyone's advice is worth hearing or heeding.

A young woman called my radio program understandably upset about her child dying. She wanted to know how to deal with the pain. This letter from Joyce is in response to that call:

"I was listening this afternoon to the young woman who, on your advice, went to her grandparents to talk to them about how to deal with the death of her infant son—as they had dealt with such an experience in their past. My husband and I are nearly ten years in our journey of grief for our little girl, Hannah, who was taken from us at age five. I feel that your advice to this young woman was right on target.

"When we found ourselves where this woman is now, we sought out folks who were farther down the journey than ourselves. It was like talking to someone who had actually made the lifeboat when we were still in the water. It was so helpful to know the thoughts and feelings we were having are common to grieving parents and were not

'unnatural.' It was so helpful to be told that, even though the pain doesn't lessen, time does make it more bearable.

"Grief is a journey. We have many more good days compared to bad days now. We no longer feel guilty to enjoy a sunset and bird singing, or family trips without her. We think of her longingly on her birthday and the anniversary of the day she left us. We went on to adopt a child who needed a family desperately and has brought so much light and love and laughter back into our lives. Our other children have gone on to live their productive lives.

"You can survive if you get the help and support, particularly from those of us who belong to this most unfortunate of fraternities.

"Thank you for your sound advice. It was profound and life-saving."

It is sometimes ferociously difficult for me to know what to say to people who call and ask, "How do I cope . . ." with terminal cancer when they have several minor children, the loss of a beloved spouse during a pregnancy, and so forth. There are generally five things I tell them:

1. There is no cure for the reality and magnitude of what has happened to them.

2. Coping will happen in phases: shock, anger, denial, depression, and then, hopefully, the ability to put thoughts and feelings in a perspective that lets them make the best out of what is left.

3. It would be good to turn to those whom they respect who have "been there—done that." If this doesn't mean

friends and relatives, then support systems of established helping groups are available.

4. Don't push away those blessings that still remain—they will give hope, solace, warmth, meaning, and strength.

5. Never underestimate the power of hugs over words.

Whine Less, Do More

Maria called my radio program wanting to know how she could repair a romantic relationship she felt she was destroying because of her jealous insecurities. He evidently does nothing in the here and now to tweak those insecurities, so it would seem that they stem largely from Maria herself.

Maria will start a fight by asking him something about a past relationship of his, he'll try to give a modest answer, and she'll just go ballistic.

Dr. Laura: My question is, what is going on inside you that would precipitate you asking him questions about his prior love life.

Maria: I believe it's paranoia and the feeling that I'm just not good enough or worthy.

Dr. Laura: Well, Maria, you just may not be! That shocked you, Maria, I'm sure. We are not worthy just because we're standing here. Some folks are nicer than others—are compassionate and sweeter, kinder, thoughtful, attentive, and caring, while others are self-centered. Wouldn't you agree?

Maria: Absolutely.

Dr. Laura: So in order to be good enough or worthy enough, we really have to work on our quality of character and our quality of behavior. So my recommendation to you, Maria, is to be the kind of woman that a man wouldn't want to leave.

Maria: Okay.

Dr. Laura: So instead of beating him up over the fact that he's had other women in the past, be the kind of woman he wants for his future. Your security does not come from him hating all other women. Your security with him or any man comes directly from giving a man what he needs from "his woman."

Maria: So then is it okay to ask someone to accept the way you are?

Dr. Laura: No, it isn't, and if he had any brains he'd leave you for the way you are now because no man needs a lifetime of this crap.

Maria: So do you think there is anything that can be said to him to convince him. . . .

Dr. Laura: No. You have to *become* the kind of woman he can feel comfortable with, admire, and respect. This is the only argument you have. You can't use your lips and promise anything . . . anybody can do that. As they say, "Talk is cheap." It's all in you walking the talk.

Maria is struggling with the issue of using *talk* to convince instead of *becoming* that which she talks about. People can live only so long on promises—and they tend to mistrust brief spurts of change. Maria may have lost this fellow, but the lesson learned is for the rest of her life. Her choice now is to continue to beat herself up over this loss, or turn it into a painful learning experience, gearing herself toward the future.

Closing Sentiment

From Tina:

"I have changed from rehasher to refresher by changing the way I enter my home. We have been married eighteen years and we love each other. I used to come home from work and complain, droning on and on ad nauseam about who did what and what I felt about it. Five years ago my husband said, 'Really, Tina, no one cares about this but you. It's too bad you're wasting our time together. We're getting older. How much time do we have left?'

"I pulled back on my hours at work, did less on projects, and generally added less to the day-to-day workload. You know what? No one did care—no one even noticed.

"Today when I enter my home, the first thing I do is to take off my 'work clothes' and put on my 'play clothes.' It's a signal to leave what should be left at work and have fun. At first I depended on Bob to set the tempo. Now I'm the one with a smile, a joke, and a kiss when Bob comes home."

Have you ever been at a party, listening to the person in front of you, when suddenly you hear something interesting behind you, and you change your focus without turning your head? Sure you have. See? You can consciously decide what voices outside and inside your head to focus on.

Make the choice toward peace and joy.

CHAPTER 3

Just Say "No" to Hurt Feelings

"I gave up the whining about fifteen years ago because IT DID NOT WORK! I was thirty and feeling old and fat and tired and sad—then I realized that I was a stay-at-home mom with two great kids and a great husband—and as long as I was making my FAMILY happy that was good enough.

"What helped me was taking ownership of my own problems. I can choose to be miserable or I can choose to be happy with what I have. I can (1) suck it up and deal with it, or (2) make the problem better and grow from it, or (3) whine about it.

"I now pick 1 or 2."

—BONNIE, A LISTENER

It is so interesting to me how many of my callers ask me, "Am I justified in having hurt/anger/disappointment over" . . . somebody doing or saying something? Or, "is it normal to feel . . . ?" It is almost as though they are asking my opinion as to whether they should or could have some particular feeling. The truth is you're going to have a particular feeling not based upon whether it is appropriate or not, but because of your unique constellation of sensitivities, experiences, personality, expectations, fears, reflex interpretations, and so forth.

Many times I might tell callers that their feelings are not reasonable. That usually makes them suck in their breath. For example, one recent caller was furious and disgusted with his seventeen-year-old-daughter, who'd been having a sexual relationship with her new stepfather. Evidently his daughter was expressing no remorse and admitted to the sex being totally consensual.

On the surface, one could understand his feelings toward her, since her behavior was immoral. Also, he was directing much of his rage at the stepfather onto his daughter, holding her accountable for their behavior. It was difficult for him to see her as his little girl anymore. He was also unknowingly angry at the loss of his fantasies about her. Knowing also that she was sexually knowledgeable with a man his own age made it difficult for him to imagine what his future relationship with her would be like. All of these emotions turned to his feeling and expression of disgust.

I said, "You know, sir, you and her mother did not hold to your vows of till death do us part, and you weren't there to raise her and her mother brought some guy into her life, their romance sexualizing her home just as she started puberty. She got you both back, didn't she? She got you both but good."

His whole tone of disgust evaporated. "Oh my gosh," he stammered. "I hadn't even thought of it that way."

"I know; that's because you were only thinking of the consequences of her sexual acting out, but not the cause: her sadness and anger at not having an intact home, and having her parents have love interests. Now she's had her first sexual experience—perhaps out of vengeance—and there's no beauty in that. She's going to need you and her mother to help her cope with this, once she thoroughly realizes what's happened, and that some man used her body without loving her."

Disgust morphed into sadness; I could hear it in his voice. Disgust and rage were gone. Those powerful feelings were shut down and replaced with compassion.

While this is an issue of perspective (see chapter 1), it is also a demonstration of how feelings can be sorted out and chosen, based upon the selection of what you choose to focus on. He could have stayed, as many callers have stayed, with his disgust, insisting, for example, that she is just a stupid girl or a slut, and he didn't raise her that way. Instead he chose to accept his responsibility as well as a rationale for her behavior that still left him with a place in her life.

When people call me seemingly asking for permission to feel a feeling, I have them explain why they imagine they have that feeling. Once they explain the circumstances they are emotionally responding to, I'll ask them if what they've told me makes sense to them. For instance, one recent caller wanted to know if she was selfish in wanting to terminate her one-year marriage (both spouses are in their late thirties) because he wants sex barely once a month and since the day of their marriage has many excuses for not being able to attain an erection.

It seems that before their wedding they were not sexually active, but she did talk about how she had a high sex drive and hoped to have sex twice a day. He had agreed to being interested in the same frequency and never told her he had preexisting erection issues.

I told her that he married her under false pretenses. She wondered why he would do that. "So, my dear, he would have company and somebody to make pb&j sandwiches."

"Yeah, I do that."

I asked her why she felt bad about herself, "selfish," when her husband intentionally misrepresented himself to trick her into marriage. "Isn't that selfish?" I asked her.

"Yes, I guess it is."

"Then why would you question yourself?"

"Because I took vows."

"You took them under his false pretenses. I actually think that kinda rescinds the contract."

You see, she felt bad about herself because she is basically a principled and decent person. Even when she is abused with lies, she still takes responsibility. That is her personality—however, that is a trait which sets people up to be preyed upon.

I suggested another, more appropriate emotion: anger.

You choose to embrace an emotion, and you have the opportunity to reject an emotion and replace it with another. As a wise person once said, recognizing that reflexive emotions happen and seem to be out of our control, still we can "Let them, like birds, land on our heads—but we don't have to let them build nests." You can, indeed, entertain a feeling, but you have the choice of what to do with it: embrace it and act on it, which might be perfectly appropriate, or dismiss it, which sometimes is a better idea. First, though, you have to understand the feeling or emotion in the context of your particular mind.

Emotions *do* have a logical basis, even if that basis is ultimately faulty. For example, someone kids you and you get all bent out of shape. We look back into your early life experiences and we see that you were quite frequently the butt of jokes and gibes because of some aspect of your family, appearance, or behavior. Having had people intending to hurt or humiliate you quite reasonably leaves you somewhat sensitive, defensive, even prickly. Perhaps you now interpret just about every playful jab as a potential blow instead of affectionate or good-natured kidding.

Based on that history, there is a certain logic to your hyperreactivity. However, defending against everything that "looks like a duck," without discerning if it really is a duck, leads you to lose out on being able to play with teddy bears and the Tickle Me Elmo kinda folks.

Perhaps as a child you felt inadequate to take care of yourself. There must come a time that you give yourself the permission to address a perceived slight to figure out *if* you should really be upset and *what* you should do about that person or situation. It probably seems an impossibility that you can choose an emotion or even reject one—feelings are generally overwhelming and apparently automatic. They are. However, that's not the end of the story. The day before I was to begin working on this chapter, I took a call from Melissa:

Melissa: Is it okay the way I am feeling or should I try to change my feelings?

Dr. Laura: What feelings are you talking about?

Melissa: Is it just wrong to feel no love and respect for my husband?

Dr. Laura: Over what have you lost love and respect for him?

She went on to tell me that they were college sweethearts, carefree, and always having fun together. He always had dreams and hopes for a career in the entertainment industry, but nothing has ever jelled. They married early and had two children, with her working to support them and managing all the finances.

Melissa: But now I've matured and I no longer accept the situation.

Dr. Laura: You married him before he had gotten a wage-earning situation?

Melissa: Yes, but I thought it would all happen.

Dr. Laura: Well, it seems like you loved him enough to join in the risk. Risk is risk—it doesn't come with a guarantee.

Melissa: Yes, I know—but . . .

Dr. Laura: Does he take care of the home?

Melissa: Well, yes, but not the way I would.

Dr. Laura: I'm not sure you'd be satisfied with my housekeeping either. Does he take care of the home in a reasonable way?

Melissa: Well, yeah.

Dr. Laura: Is he taking care of the children?

Melissa: Yes.

Dr. Laura: Is he a good daddy?

Melissa: Yes.

Dr. Laura: Okay, Melissa, here it is: you are entitled to be disappointed that your mutual dreams never came to fruition—you can turn them into disdain and dislike. You have that ability and you have that choice.

Imagine for a moment coming into that home without him there having created a home out of a house, without the children there because they're on fifty-fifty visitation, without somebody caring each day whether you're alive or dead, without his support for all you go through in your endeavors. Imagine life without him—that man you don't love and respect. Imagine.

The next sound I heard was Melissa crying. Yes, it's true, she didn't have the pretty picture they'd both painted years ago—but she did have another pretty picture. She saw at that moment that she could choose her emotion: gratitude, relief, love, and affection or resentment, disappointment, and disgust.

Her tears and sniffling told me that she chose the former. She thanked me and hung up quietly.

There is no life without disappointment and loss—things just don't always go as planned or hoped for, or even needed. If life is like a salad, I always yank out the olives, onions, and nuts. I don't rant about them existing—I just do what I need to do to make the salad a pleasure. Focus on an olive—and you may scrunch up your face all the time. Focus on the romaine lettuce and Parmesan cheese, and you smile all the way to your main dish. You get to choose.

Behavior Invites Feelings

A brief e-mail from Rose, a listener, shows you how easy it sometimes is to shift feelings.

"What helped me replace whining with a life of doing was when, fifteen years ago, I made a call to Dr. Laura. As she listened as I whined to her about my crummy parents and how I wanted to clear my name by ruining their reputation, her clarity forced me to see that I was choosing gossip over living an honorable life.

"At times it was very lonely living honorably instead of gossiping. Occasionally I wished for everyone to rally around my victimness instead. But I would imagine Dr. Laura saying, 'The more you do the right thing, the easier life is.'

"These two Dr. Laura-isms changed my life:

1. *The less I act on a feeling, the less I feel it.*

2. *Taking control is a no-brainer when 'doing the right thing' comes before my desires.*

"Fifteen years later, I can say that living honorably is much more rewarding than I ever imagined it could be."

Upset feelings would lead us to behaviors of either retaliation, self-abuse, or perpetual rumination—if we let them. Any of those behaviors feed back into growing those upset feelings and letting them take solid root.

I remember in college seeing a coffee mug with the quote "Don't let the bastards get you down." I was really taken by that. It had always seemed like there was one and only one progression from upset feelings (hurt or anger) and that was to fight back. It took me a while to realize that I could choose my battles and that there was a distinct and important difference between retaliation and demanding justice.

Retaliation promotes negativity, while justice encourages more positive thoughts and emotions, even if the justice is neither immediate nor forthcoming at all. The journey of trying to "set things *right*" has our psyche more involved in striving for good than retaliation, which generally directs us to up the ante on someone else's pain, which never really makes us feel better for very long.

Another coffee mug saying that has motivated me is "The best revenge is living well." In my very public position and talking about moral choices and ethical behavior, I am perpetually attacked, maligned, insulted, misrepresented, and outright lied about by folks who disagree with my opinions and positions. They don't debate; they attempt to assassinate. I won't kid you, it is upsetting. People have even focused on hurting my son as a way to hurt me—imagine how that feels! I have always done my best to set the record straight (a form of justice), but do not retaliate in kind because that would only warp my soul. I remember the lessons from my childhood with bullies looking to see if you flinch or blink. When you appeared unfazed, they stepped back and looked for another target that would better feed their sadistic need for power by cowering.

And the truth is, from my own experience, the less you behave like you care, the less you come to care. The less you care, the more you can stay on track with your personal mission and the more frustrated the bad guys become because their mission is destruction. Your happiness thwarts that.

You are probably not a public person, but I know, from thirty years of callers, that everyone has a share of bullies and bad situations. Actually forcing yourself to behave as though you are untouched in the storm truly leaves you feeling less touched.

The behavior always precedes the feelings—either negative or positive. Do not sit around and wait for bad feelings to abate before you start living your life fully. That is a huge mistake way too many people make: putting their lives on hold—and the joy they could experience—until such time as those feelings stop. You can stop the feelings, or at least attenuate them greatly, by doing the things that make life worth living for you and others.

Editing Out the Bad

If you keep just being "reactive" to disappointments and slights, your life deteriorates dramatically. Katherine, a listener, wrote about this:

"Over the last couple of years I have come to the realization that I don't like the person I'm becoming. Don't get me wrong. I do a lot of things right, but my nature has been to always see the downside of things.

"I recently decided to edit out my complaining and whining. The problem is that I don't have much to say. My whole identity had become wrapped up in the complaining. I know my husband hates to hear it, so I started with improving my conversations with him.

"Let me tell you that I am struggling to keep the conversations going. I know it will take time to find the positive replacements for my previously negative way of thinking—but I'm sure my husband won't mind a month or two of more quiet."

Now it just might be that Katherine has a lot of ugly stuff constantly happening to her. If that is so, you might think her justified in detailing the painful emotions she has in response to the yucky situations. While that may be true, what kind of life is that? What kind of friend or spouse will stay in your life long when you are but a spigot of perpetually flowing negativity?

One recent caller, who barely knew the woman he married,

called me one year into the marriage complaining that she was getting fat (she had gained twenty-five pounds at that point), wouldn't exercise or diet, and was totally nonaffectionate, the last having been the case throughout their brief courtship.

Of course he wanted to know how to change her. I said that he couldn't. He'd have to accept that she'll likely get fatter and be even less affectionate over time. He felt guilty leaving her, as he'd already had a few failed relationships and marriages.

He wanted to know how he was supposed to cope with the fat and lack of affection.

When people ask me "how to cope," they generally mean, "How do I live with this when my feelings are so negative?" My answer is always the same: accept or stop fighting what *is* and wrap your emotional world around the aspects of the person or the situation about which you are pleased and/or grateful.

You "edit out the bad."

Time to Let It Go

Susan's letter indicates she knew "what time it was" for her: *"In this culture we are encouraged to find and lay blame for our personal shortcomings/minor deprivations. We embrace and even celebrate our 'victimized' selves. I had my own 'excuses'; they relieved me of the responsibility for my life.*

"One day, when I was about thirty years old, I was whining about my parents. I was in a small group of women, one of whom was not my favorite person. In the middle of my self-pitying rant,

Cathy interrupted me and said, 'Aren't you a little OLD to still be complaining about your parents?'

"I considered rejecting her remark because I didn't particularly like the source and she was, after all, taking away my 'excuse' for my life. However, there was a flash of recognition and a horrible truth in what she said and I was appropriately chagrined.

"Remembering how it felt to be 'called out' like that, I was forever aware when I was tempted to try to 'go back there.' Grow up, Susan!"

Part of maturing is letting go. Some people call that process "forgiveness"; I do not. "Letting go" is something you do because without doing it, you cannot in any healthy way move on to higher levels of thinking, feeling, interacting, and giving to others.

One recent female caller was complaining in high speed about her mother's lifelong mean behavior. Actually, it was more than mean—it was destructive: false accusations, browbeatings, starting hideous rumors, and such. I listened carefully and quietly to that caller, and when I finally had an opportunity, I told her that I thought she was in no way ready to be married.

Boy oh boy, was she ever stunned by my turning it back on her! I told her that while she was still struggling with a sick relationship with a dangerous parent, she was in no way available for a healthy marriage.

The rest of the conversation didn't go well. While I tried to make the point that she had to "let go" of her mother, she fought back by saying, "Oh, I have." To that I replied, "Then you wouldn't be on the phone with me right now."

Ouch.

I certainly understand how difficult it is for people to give up on their hopes, dreams, and fantasies—especially about a mommy or a daddy—but as difficult as it might be, it sometimes must be done for the sake of your present and future well-being.

Sadly, some parents are just jerks, while others are outright cruel, and still others are manipulative and greedy. Normal responses to this usually include feelings of guilt, anger, and sadness. Those are the ingredients of depression and, all too often, are dealt with by punishing a spouse or children, withholding love and affection, or inflicting self-abuse.

No matter who the individual(s)—parents, siblings, friends, coworkers, bosses, neighbors, or even children—there comes a time when you must "let it go." That may or may not mean those individuals are out of your life; it could just be that you let go of your negative emotions for your own well-being.

This is probably one of the most difficult concepts of this book. This is usually the place in which I get the most arguments from callers: "But, but I'm worried that…," or "But it isn't fair that…," or, "I'm just supposed to accept that . . . " And my answer is typically, "Look, nothing is going to change. You have no say or control. Do you want to continue being miserable or would you rather find a way to coexist?"

Every person or situation generally has good and bad going for it. Unless the bad is dangerous or destructive, edit it out and embrace the good. No, it won't be perfect, but it won't be made perfect no matter how much you decide to continue to suffer anyway!

Switch Back Out of That Dark Place

"I was listening to your program when you had a caller who confessed to overeating and overspending. The minute I heard this, I focused all of my attention onto what you had to say. I am guilty of both and yet have been too afraid of what you would say to call you myself.

"You were so calm and encouraging when talking to her. You asked what she felt before doing either (eating or spending) and what made her feel that way in her earlier life.

"I asked myself the same questions; for the first time, I realized I felt sad and alone at times, and also realized it stems from childhood and my own parents' divorce when I was four. I am almost thirty years old now. I am happily married to a wonderful man and wonderful father to our three very healthy and wonderful little boys. I am very happy, loved, and FULL. They are my happiness. I am NOT alone, or sad—except when I allow myself to 'switch' back to that place.

"I realize I am in control of my reaction and behavior that follows those feelings. I also realize that I now do have everything I wanted as a child. I have the happy home and family. There is no need to keep looking for that. What I HAVE is everything I NEED."

It's hard for me to imagine what I can add to Sabrina's letter— so let me just resort to a bit more clarification. When you have missed out on certain necessities of early childhood, like love, affection, and attention from parents in a reasonably happy, intact home, there is always a "hole in your heart." Like a hole in the sidewalk, it is easy to fall into and repeatedly sprain your ankle. What Sabrina did was to finally recognize that while history cannot be revised, the present is giving her the blessings she once longed for.

She has chosen to be happy about today, and to wrench herself out of the sadness of yesterday in order to enjoy that happiness.

Somehow telling people to "count their blessings" tends to get them angry, as though that phrase, though trite by now, had no merit or wisdom. What makes it so difficult for you to accept what is light, when the darkness is so oppressive? One would think that you'd enthusiastically jump toward the light! The answer is simple, really—you don't want there to be darkness; you want to conquer, punish, or eliminate the darkness. Generally, none of that is possible.

Searching for the light is a better way. Switch from cursing the darkness to celebrating the light.

Compassion for Others Trumps Negative Feelings

I am always impressed by the magnificent displays of humanity that callers express on my program or write to me about. Tami is one of those remarkable people:

"I caught the end of a call from a woman whose mother criticized her nonworking (laid off) husband a lot. You explained to her that her husband was hurt and it was hard on him to be home instead of working and taking care of his family—and she needed to concentrate on her family and stop crying over her mother's comments.

"My husband just went back to work last November 2006 after being on worker's comp due to a back injury. He was out of work for two and a half years. We have a five-year-old son. Let me tell you,

*I went to work EVERY day! I came home and made dinner, I did
laundry on the weekend, and I gave my son his nightly bath after
helping him with his homework.*

"*My husband went through his bouts of depression, and when
he did, I loved him and told him it wasn't his fault that he got hurt
and that it wouldn't be forever.*

"*He had two surgeries and countless hours of physical therapy. He
was already suffering enough and he didn't need me to be whining
about how tired I was. He was there to pick up our son every day
after school and took him to the park in the afternoon. He did what
he could to help around the house, but with his injury, it was hard.*

"*Finally he is back to work and he has completely changed in
that he smiles now and is very happy. It was hard for him to be
stuck at home and have his wife be the breadwinner, but I never,
never complained and I made sure I went out of my way to tell him
how proud I am of how quickly he got back to work and that he is
doing a great job.*

"*My husband always thanks me for not putting him down and
for not making him feel like less of a man because he was unable to
work.*"

There is no way in the world that Tami was not overwhelmed,
frustrated, annoyed, stressed out, and irritated by the situation.
Instead of becoming consumed by that quite understandable
constellation of emotions, she used her compassionate love for
her husband to buoy both their spirits. This is another example of
how wonderfully things are endured and worked through when
you care more about the other person than you care to feel sorry
for yourself.

Too many marriages and relationships in general tend to have a large competitive aspect to them. Competitiveness crushes compassion. When you have to be right or in control or look superior or generally just "better than," there is no room for compassion. Competitiveness precludes sensitivity to the needs and feelings of others. Compassion for others is like a warm blanket over your own soul.

Remember the old saying "I wept because I had no shoes until I saw a man who had no feet"? Say no to self-indulgent wallowing, and bring your touch to someone else's heart.

Reframe the Negative into a Positive

Lynne, a listener, reflected on the complaining of some young women callers that their breasts were too small and they wanted breast enhancement plastic surgery. She mused that they thought having *fake* breasts would boost their self-esteem.

"I am a two-time breast cancer survivor. I have had two radical mastectomies and have NO breasts at all. Due to the severity of my cancer, my doctors recommended against reconstruction. Regarding my body: I LOVE my body. My husband LOVES my body. Instead of breasts I have two large scars; scars that spell life, scars that remind me every day how precious our time is on this planet.

"When I was young and had a gash on my arm, my mother said, 'No one will pay any more attention to that scar than you do.' She was right and it applies every day to my chest. I pay no attention and my husband pays no attention. These girls could use this same lesson.

"I want to tell these young women that they are not who they are

because of the size of their breasts. They are who they are because of
their attitude toward life. I am very successful and attractive. I have
many, many friends, business colleagues, and loved ones who do not
give one hoot about my breastless body."

What is reframed here? Ugly scars, reminders of frightening
cancer, are reframed as evidence that there is still life; with
life comes opportunities to enjoy family, friends, activities . . .
just breathing in the smell of garden flowers or a child's newly
shampooed hair.

It is easy to see how one could become glued to the fear of
death. But even here, at the gateway to a possible painful death,
you can see the surgical scars as the openings to hell or as the road
sign "More life and love ahead"!

Squash That Negative Seed Before It Sprouts

The most difficult moment to imagine cutting a bad feeling
off at the pass is the instant it swells inside your chest and makes
a beeline for your gut and head. You feel as though you are
consumed and completely out of control. In fact, that's pretty
accurate, but it is not the end of the story.

There is always a "thought" that precedes the uncomfortable
or upsetting feeling. You may not be completely aware of that
at the time you are struck with an emotion. That's why, at
calmer moments, it's good to look back and try to dissect out the
triggering thought. It is this thought that usually has to be dealt
with, not the feeling that it provokes.

Stephanie's e-mail talks more generically about this phenomenon:

"I wasn't a huge complainer, but I definitely saw the negative in things too often, which led to complaining. I realized that it started with a negative thought about something or someone in my head and just spiraled from there.

"I discovered that if I caught myself in the beginning, and decided to think of all the wonderful things about that person or situation, I stopped the rapid decline toward complaining.

"It's not always easy and many times I just plain don't want to do it. But I do it anyway.

"In time, you truly start to see the person or situation in a different light. In turn, you can focus your energy toward your family. A specific example of where this has helped me has been with my husband. The embarrassing part of it is that I realized he is one of the most unselfish, hardworking, easygoing individuals out there. I think I already knew that—but still chose to complain about small things and nitpick. Shame on me."

I generally ask callers who are complaining or whining about somebody or some situation if indeed it is an "event" or a "pattern." When it is a pattern, then continuing to whine precludes making decisions that they really don't want to have to make. Why don't they? It is difficult to give up on dreams, fantasies, and hopes; it is embarrassing to imagine the "I told you so" remarks you'd have to bear; and it is way too exasperating to imagine starting again with somebody or something new. The devil we know seems to have a leg up on the devil we don't know; nonetheless, I remind callers that it might be an angel we're opening ourselves up for.

When it is an event, it is easier to quash the reflex emotional reaction because you simply have to remind yourself that whatever it is might have some explanation we haven't thought of. If you've had all good experiences with people or situations, then please, give them the benefit of the doubt and rely on your past knowledge of their character and intentions toward you.

Things are not always as they seem, and when your insecurities or fears overwhelm your judgment and patience, you might condemn and ultimately damage or push away in retaliation for your perceived hurt, when it wasn't necessary at all.

Sometime things are exactly what they seem; however, the history you have with that person or situation may help you forgive and repair without loss.

The problem I have with too many callers is a seeming desire to hold on to the hurt and anger. Some callers have said, in their defense, "Well, if I seem to let it go, then they'll just think I'm easy," or "I want them to know just how much they hurt me," or "I want to make sure they hurt as much as I did," or "I don't want to let them off the hook lest they think they can get away with this or something else."

I'm sure all those reading that last paragraph recognized themselves at some point in their lives. These are pretty natural concerns and points of view. However, they are ultimately self-defeating. As I have told many a spouse, "If you are going to continue to keep up that wall and torture them, you might as well end the relationship. It won't have a future anyway. And your continued negative thoughts and actions will only serve to make you more bitter—definitely not more happy. That's not a life I'd want to commit to."

You Are What You Give

Whining and suffering are a safe place to be. You'll get sympathy and they serve to protect you from further hurt or disappointment. The downside is that you stop living. Living includes ups and downs to celebrate or endure, disappointments and frustrations to overcome, triumphs and failures to balance, and love and loss to grow from.

Lorna, another listener, learned that from listening to one of my callers:

"I am a believer that things happen for a reason, so when you opened the show with an e-mail update from the day before, I was not surprised to hear of the woman who was afraid to be intimate with (or nice to) her husband.

"My situation is a little different in that I am afraid to be intimate with my husband (I think because I am afraid of losing him) and so I create ways to keep space (both literal and emotional) between us.

"I heard you speak to the woman who said she is married to a wonderful man whom she does not treat well because of the dynamic her parents were in and what she learned from witnessing them. You walked her through why she is mimicking their relationship and explained that it is not necessary—because she chose better!

"As you spoke to her, I imagined you were speaking to me. I asked myself, 'Why am I afraid of being close to the wonderful man that I chose? And by not allowing the intimacy, what am I losing out on?' I decided that when I got home and saw my husband, I would go against my usual tendency to be stiff and standoffish.

I would really listen to him, hug and kiss him and show him the attention he deserves.

"Dr. Laura, I was surprised by the immediate gratification I felt. My love for him grew like the heart inside the Grinch when he sees what doing good things for others can do for you. And finally, I do not feel guilty anymore for not being enough. I am so glad I heard that call and took your advice."

Imagining that you're safe from negative judgment and therefore rejection or loss by shooting before you see the whites of their eyes is obviously very self-defeating. Your very act of self-protection makes others value you and connect to you less.

When asked about what it is that people can say or do to make other people like them, I always say, "Other people will like you if you simply show them that you like and are interested in them. It isn't some performance that will attract them—that will only entertain them. When you come out of yourself enough to show them that they are interesting and matter . . . it's like blowing in their ear."

So instead of whining about every little thing to justify your resistance of the yin and yang of life, jump right in: usually the water is fine, and when it's not, that's what friends and loved ones are for.

Closing Sentiment

I've spent a lot of time watching the National Geographic and Discovery channels. There is so much to learn from the dynamics of animal behavior—even from sharks.

Ben wrote,

"I am a forty-three-year-old-firefighter/paramedic. Eighteen years ago when I was a rookie, I had no idea what a testosterone-filled environment the firehouse could be. From my first day in the firehouse, I was tested by my coworkers to see if I had a breaking point. I was picked on, ridiculed, and belittled. I thought I was handling the attacks well, but all the time I was secretly considering quitting my career (whining). It was a hard decision because I devoted years in school and eighteen weeks of an academy to earn my right to be in the firehouse (or so I thought).

"One afternoon the station lieutenant called me into his office. He had noticed I was becoming angry with my fellow firemen. That's when he told me something I will never forget. He handed me a trifold brochure he had picked up from a SCUBA dive shot. It was entitled, 'How to Swim with Sharks.' He asked me to open it and read aloud from the section on what not to do. It said, '#1 Don't Bleed!' He then explained how life in the firehouse could be like swimming with sharks. The attacks were making me bleed and I was putting the whole firehouse into a feeding frenzy. He told me to laugh in their faces when they picked on me and to show them my indifference by asking, 'That's the best you could come up with?'

"At first, I was just saying the words, but eventually I became more confident and the attacks stopped when I gained their respect. Today I am so glad I didn't give up and quit my career. At times I am humbled by the thought of being included with such extraordinary people as the firemen I work with.

"From time to time I've met a rookie who looks like he might be reaching his own breaking point. When that happens I bring out my old trifold brochure and have him read aloud. . . ."

Not only do the military, police, firemen, and such need to know that the person watching their back is strong enough to face all emotional obstacles with guts and tenacity; everyone you have a relationship with will test you at some point to make sure he or she can count on you. I know that I have had many therapy sessions as well as on-air conversations with folks who insult and argue and fight with me—all to test whether I have what it takes to help them bear their pain and real or imagined sins.

If the person in your life is simply abusive, destructive, or dangerous, it's time for you to find the door. Most of the time, though, you're experiencing the growing pains of relationship and group dynamics. Don't whine, don't bleed. Face it all with ever-growing self-confidence and strength that you can get only from experience.

CHAPTER 4

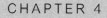

Always So Sa-a-a-a-a-d

"In spite of abandonment by our father, ongoing molestation by a 'trusted' family member, school yard taunting for being a 6'3" girl by the age of fourteen . . . I AM HAPPY! My secret? My stepdad. We were not allowed to whine about anything. When riding in a car for hours, if I were to start complaining in my little girl, whiny voice, 'IIIII'm thiiiirsty!,' my stepdad would jovially reply, 'I'm Don. Nice to meet you, Thirsty!' His motto was 'No whiners on this bus!'

"I once asked him how he could get over a past like his (beatings, poverty, an alcoholic dad). He grabbed me in a hug, smiled in my face, and said, 'Cause look at everything I have now!'

"No whining on this bus!"

—ASHLEY, A LISTENER

S adly, sadness is an inherent part of life. There are innumerable tragedies, accidents, problems, disappointments, frustrations, offenses, losses, betrayals, challenges, diseases, and wars, as well as strife, hatred, bad luck, and random acts of malevolence that make everyday life some level of struggle for every human being on the planet. Opportunities for suffering and sadness are the one universal constant for all humanity.

There is no such miracle as a life with all blessings, and as you all have been told a zillion times, life isn't fair. In October 2007 arson fires ignited much of the California coast from San Diego to Malibu. What was truly amazing is how in some neighborhoods you'd see most homes leveled to the ground, with smoke still rising from the embers, while one home in the middle of the conflagration would be still standing like a ghost that would not concede defeat in the face of the raging flames.

Frankly, whining about it—even yelling, screaming, or raging about it—sounds like a reasonable response to an unreasonable situation, and for a limited time perhaps even a healthy response. I've said on the air many times in response to callers wondering how or why they should give up the whining, "I reserve the right to whine, bitch, and moan for maybe two or three days. It's like a body throwing up tainted food; the poison has to be let out before the recovery and healing may commence. Whining has its place in that same way."

For many, four-letter words do the trick. However, like whining, overuse of cursing gets you only so far in reestablishing the equilibrium that lets you continue to live with some contentment or satisfaction. The main problem with staying in the whining mode is that it creates a state of mind that seems to dig you deeper into your sadness hole. The more you contemplate, relive, and curse the hurt, the more miserable you grow to feel, and the more you become immune to acknowledging the good in your life.

Some of you get very angry when told to "count your blessings." I know, I know. It's like an insult to you. It suggests that you shouldn't be unhappy at all because there are good things happening today and tomorrow. You're right. The timing of that "truth" is a delicate issue. Let me be clear: I think you're entitled to your reasonable sadness—don't let anybody take that away from you. If you don't feel the feelings—even the most miserable of them—it's like having a gear jam in your head and heart. Acknowledging the feelings is the lubricant you require to make sure that you function appropriately no matter what the situation or predicament. When it is sadness you feel: FEEL IT! Acknowledge it, talk about it, let it have a *temporary* home in your life. And then it must go someplace for storage—

not ignored or denied, but also not held in a death-grip embrace.

Sadness takes on many disguises. Sometimes it looks like tears and moping—that form is very obvious—but most of the time it takes the shape of insecurity, fears, anxieties, even anger—and, very often, stupid behavior.

Karen's letter is such a great example of this:

"A few years ago a friend suggested that I listen to your program. At the time I was trying to justify staying in an abusive relationship that I had engaged in when both my children moved out of state after high school.

"I was suffering from depression, empty-nest syndrome, and mostly stupidity. I tried to listen to your show but found you annoying, kind of mean, and not all that wise.

"Flash forward to now. I am no longer in the abusive relationship. After three stints in a mental hospital and two suicide attempts I finally decided to face my two biggest fears: being alone and being accountable for my actions. Neither has been easy, but what has helped me through a lot of tough times is your show. I no longer find you annoying and I almost always agree with your advice. You haven't changed—so I guess I have.

"I am trying daily to be a good person, mother, and soon-to-be grandmother. I thank God every day for allowing me to maintain a relationship with my children and for the wisdom to be a good grandmother.

"I can see myself in so many of your callers—I just wish I would have given you more of a chance years ago."

Karen's sadness from losing her role as mommy when the chicks flew the nest is normal. Her response to this normal reaction was destructive. She was so desperate to avoid being alone that she hooked up with someone who wanted and needed her. It was probably a quick hookup, driven by her need for someone and his need to control someone.

I'm sure that Karen spent a lot of time being sad and complaining to friends about her situation. What she needed was the willingness to be alone—and the necessity of taking control... what she called "being accountable for her actions."

Hence, the title of this book, *Stop Whining, Start Living.*

It is also not unusual for people in her predicament of a mixture of denial, fear, and shunning personal responsibility to find me and my message quite annoying. When you're whining, it's about someone else's responsibilities to you; when you listen to me, it's about you taking responsibility for yourself. It sometimes seems curious that people will rebel when I'm trying to give them their own power—and they push it away. That's because it is so difficult to travel the land of the unknown; too often, the ugly known seems more appealing than the beautiful unknown. I try to tip the scales back.

Extricating from Ancient Suffering

Angie didn't call to tell me she was sad; not directly, anyway. She called to ask me, "Can you help me to begin to change from a person who is insecure and self-centered into a person with substance?"

Dr. Laura: Sure. Self-centeredness is attention turned inward. The more time you contemplate your own navel, the more you'll stay insecure and self-involved. The more time you contemplate greater things and other people's navels, the less insecure you'll be about yourself because you're just not going to have time to think about it.

Angie: Okay.

Dr. Laura: I mean, it's just natural. You've noticed that you've had some days where you wake up and you're either nervous or upset and you don't know exactly why? But somebody asks you to do a favor and you just rush out and take care of business and you're not thinking of yourself anymore. You're not suffering over your stuff—you're occupied!

Angie: Yeah, it feels good.

Dr. Laura: Yeah! And while you're occupied and somebody looks at you and says, "Oh, thank you. You're just a lifesaver," you feel great. So it comes down to how we spend our emotional time.

Angie: But what if you are a "people pleaser"? I've heard you say that that is ultimately self-centered behavior because it focuses in on making people like you . . . right?

Dr. Laura: Yes, you're quite right. People-pleasing behavior is nothing about giving—it's all about getting safety from criticism, anger, or rejection and ensuring being "liked." However, the people-pleaser is usually quite sad much of the time with a "martyr" identity: I do for others and still don't get back what I need.

People-pleasers start out as people who are sad about their

worth and lovability. They have come to see themselves not very positively and manipulate to try to feel okay.

Angie: I get confused between being a people-pleaser and really helping others.

Dr. Laura: There's a difference. Kissing butt is different from really helping somebody.

Angie: I get it.

Dr. Laura: Do you want to read to the blind? Or do you want to eat dirt from your family so nobody will yell at you?

Angie: That sounds familiar.

I then spent some time, believe it or not, only on how airily (breathily) she spoke. I told her that she wasn't sitting up straight, that she sounded like a beaten-down puppy—all scared. She responded, "This happens to me when I get really nervous." I told her that even if she were nervous or afraid, she didn't have to give in to that whispering, quiet voice.

Angie: Do you know . . . you're right. Because people always ask me to repeat what I've said.

Dr. Laura: Yes, because you mumble. And you mumble because if they hear you, you might get in trouble! If you make a statement you'd have to stand behind it and maybe risk their disapproval.

Angie: Yup.

It may sound strange to you for me to include a discussion about people-pleasing and whispering in a book about whining and sadness. After all, neither Angie nor I ever actually even used the word "sadness" throughout the entire call. We didn't have to. When people cower to others it definitely does come from a sad place of feeling powerless, unsafe, incompetent, inferior, and unlovable, owing to the aforementioned. It's a vicious circle.

My assignment to her was to simply speak louder all the time, even in prayer. I told her to let herself be heard and take the risks because she needed to be "somebody." People-pleasers are nobody in particular—just what others want them to be. To be somebody you have to take up space: be seen, heard, and reckoned with. There is an inherent sadness in not being your own man or woman lest you be punished or rejected.

Getting attention is central to human existence. Sometimes you go about it in all the wrong ways.

Babies Cry to Get Attention— I Can Too!

Jennifer, a listener, wrote about learning the power of whining to get that attention: *"My parents divorced when I was five. After that, I was ignored unless I whined loud enough and long enough to attract attention. I carried that into my early adulthood."*

Coincidentally, right after receiving this letter I took a call from a woman who said, oddly, that she wanted to know how to stop sabotaging her successes. Generally when people ask that question, the problem has something to do with issues of accountability, ultimate failure, and so forth. This situation was way different.

When I asked her what she thought was at the core of her concerns about success, she said, "I won't be loved."

What? People usually think that they'll be loved if they are perfect and/or do everything perfectly. This was a real surprise. So I questioned her further about her childhood. After being somewhat evasive, she finally told me that her parents were busy people and they basically responded to her only when she was bad—so she was "bad" a lot.

I told her that she was obviously a very sad little girl who has grown up into a very confused young woman.

Dr. Laura: You weren't being loved. You were being disciplined. Since that was most of the attention you ever got, you needed to redefine your parents' mobilization in response to your crises as love. Without that, your sadness would have overwhelmed you completely.

Mary: I never quite saw it that way.

Dr. Laura: You're bringing the wrong horse to the race. Failing is not the fast track to love—being loving is. Love is what you get when you give. Success is a separate issue. And success doesn't get you love. It might get you respect and admiration by some, jealousy and resentment by others.

Love, Mary, is what you already get from your husband and children because you give and sacrifice for them. So whatever it is that you wish to do that you deem an action toward success, leave the "love stuff" out of it. It's a different horse.

• • •

People carry all sorts of misunderstandings from their childhood into their adulthood. Even though a child's mind processes things differently from an adult's (children's conceptualizations being rather concrete and simplistic), those notions do persist and do impact the adult's ability to function with the freedom and wisdom of age and experience.

I took a call one day from a husband and wife who had been married fourteen years and had five children. They were on the precipice of divorce because they couldn't come together to be and give what the other needed. Why? Their childhood perceptions.

It turns out the husband's mother was a mean alcoholic who constantly bad-mouthed the divorced dad and was a demanding, hyperemotional caricature of a woman. This resulted in a husband becoming almost immune to the emotional demands of a woman. Hence, when his wife was emotionally needy, as when her sister was dying, he was quite mechanical about the issues of financing the trip to the hospital and then to the funeral. This obviously hurt her deeply—and this was the sort of thing that was going on for the full fourteen years.

The wife had been brought up in a home in which the emotional needs of the children were pretty much ignored—as though the children were invisible. This resulted in a wife who never believed her needs would be acknowledged, much less met. She married a man who would fulfill that prophecy and they would disappoint each other forever.

Once I pointed out the dynamics between them, I instructed them not to make huge or quick changes in order to "save this marriage," since that would be too jarring for either of them to bear. She not only had to get used to expressing her feelings, but had to be clearly instructive as to how he might meet them without escalating to the point at which his "mother aversion" got into gear. He had to get used to responding to her emotions in a loving, sensitive way without overwhelming her ability to be vulnerable.

These changes are not easy to make, and need a lot of reinforcement. I asked them to call me from time to time for a "rebooting."

People like this couple can stay sad for decades of their lives, feeling as though they are doomed to never be happy or give happiness enough to make a difference simply because they don't understand that the dynamics have less to do with today and more to do with their personal yesterday. When that is so, you naturally tend to blame the other person for some lack.

If you think you might recognize yourself in this predicament, please read my *Bad Childhood—Good Life*. In it you are likely to get more insight into your childhood dynamic and learn how to get unstuck.

Reasonable Sadness

I recently took a heartbreaking call from a woman who is thirty-six, is married, has one two-year-old, and has had eleven miscarriages. That's not the sadness she was calling about. The sadness was that she discovered she was about six weeks pregnant. Her sadness is that she can't be happy, regrets being pregnant, and won't go to the doctor or even tell her husband because doing so would make, she feels, the ugly past come up and consume her again.

I told her that some part of her did indeed wish to try again—that was the part that didn't use birth control. I also had her call her husband via a landline while I was on her cell phone. She balked at first at telling him; again, this would make it real and a prospective rerun of past horrors. I told her she had no right to withhold this from him:

- It was his child, too.

- She was his concern.

- His feelings mattered.

- He was part of the coping scenario.

She calmed down and agreed to call him. He was surprised, hopeful, and sensitive. I then told her she had a moral obligation to behave as if she never had a prior problem with a pregnancy because doing other than that might impact the pregnancy—and should it go to term without medical support, vitamins, etc., she'd possibly regret it. Additionally, she was missing out on the joy she'd finally have after all those failures.

Finally, I told her to drop the sadness, since this pregnancy had gone weeks past all the prior miscarriages and no blessing should be held at arm's length because of past disappointments.

The next day BrieAnne sent this e-mail:

"I just got done drying my tears after listening to the lady who found out she was pregnant and was having a hard time being happy about it. I just want to say that I went through a similar situation where I just wasn't ready for my second child. I was even pushed to get an abortion by my own grandmothers—which I immediately refused.

"I cried a lot and was way more upset about it than being happy. My dear husband was my rock and helped me throughout my pregnancy. Throughout my complications I was able to give him the ultimate gift of his son on Christmas Eve.

"Now I look at our baby and wonder how I could have ever been so sad. Thank you for giving that caller encouragement and hopefully she, like me, will look at her baby and never remember the feeling of that sadness again."

As I write this section I'm worrying that you might think I take sad feelings lightly—you know, a "just buck up" attitude. I can assure you that I don't take your sadness or mine lightly! There are many situations that make sadness a reasonable place—it's just not a reasonable home address.

Sa-a-a-adness Is a Choice

How can sadness possibly be a choice? How can you possibly pull yourself out of that hole? Isn't it even cruel and insensitive to suggest somebody just stop being sad or depressed?

Jasbir has a personal opinion on this:

"I have to many degrees recently changed my life from complaining, self-pity, and lack of action to one of a life of causative action and handling my issues directly and living my life with much more energy and zest.

"The biggest thing that helped me make this transition was that I just made the decision not to be in an almost state of depression and take life by the horns and start taking care of my stuff and doing every little thing on a day-to-day basis to make my life better.

"After going through a period of about three years of just plain self-pity, I have dramatically changed my life in about six months. I am still digging myself out of the financial hole I dug for myself, but my personal life is much better, as is my communication with my significant other even though we live apart. Even the time I spend with my kids now is much more constructive. Pitfalls were the confronting of all the things I had neglected."

There they are yet again: the notions of being constructive, confronting things neglected, and being held accountable for one's own decisions, actions, and inactions.

Admittedly, one of the most difficult things to do is get active when you feel sad and depressed. By definition, you have no energy, hope, motivation, or desire to do anything you already know would make you feel better.

When I was in private practice (Marriage and Family Therapy) I would use subtle tactics to get the sad individual somewhat angry at something in life—or even me. That surge of adrenaline was a godsend, as it would lift the person out of that black pit into a raging red tunnel with some light at the end.

There are other methods to help a person lift from sadness; this letter is from Debby:

"The other day my husband noticed that I was very sad. He tried to cheer me up but it wasn't working well. So he whispered in my ear with a grin on his face that there would be a 'BIG' surprise that night. But there was a catch: I had to be cheery all day!

"Several times through the day he'd ask something and I'd answer him and add at the end 'And that was very cheery' or 'And I'm being VERY cheery' with a smile. His ear-to-ear grin told me how much he appreciated my disposition and anticipated our evening.

"After dinner, doing the dishes, I made a comment again, 'And I'm being very cheery.'" I heard my six-year-old say, 'Why are you being so cheery? You are never like that!'

"Oh, out of the mouths of babes! I'd spent the past several months being out of sorts with several things and had NO idea how much everyone else had noticed. I swallowed hard and answered, 'But I'm cheery now—very cheery!'

"I learned an important lesson: how smart my husband is! He changed my mood without saying one negative thing. And . . . I'm cheery today too!"

Actually, her husband being "smart" was a lovely observation, but I don't think that was the most important lesson to be learned through her experience. Probably the most important lesson is that moods are not constructed of, forgive the expression, Krazy Glue! Moods come and moods go. Moods stay around when we embrace them or have a psychiatric disorder that requires psychotropic medication—and that is the exception and not the rule regardless of all the television commercials that make all moods the target of chemical intervention rather than coping and striving.

We embrace moods when we're afraid of the alternatives. Yes, a switch to a positive mood can seem threatening if you believe you don't deserve it, it won't get you redress for whatever hurt you've experienced, you will lose sympathy and caretaking that you desperately desire, and so forth.

It is a test of maturity and grit to confront a mood and reject it. Just the other day I experienced a surprise setback. I immediately became emotionally upset, turned on my heels, and decided to take my marbles and go home. Yeah, I did that. I was bummed out, sad, and hurt, and this was my way of striking back.

When I was most of the way home I felt ferocious guilt for seeming a bad sport, and generally felt like an idiot for letting some people down by leaving them with the situation. I came back and apologized to everyone. I said, "Okay, I'm finished pouting—let's get back into this and take it on and show them what we're made of!"

All the folks were impressed that I pulled my act together, owned the babyishness of my response, took responsibility, apologized, and got back into warrior gear. I must admit, I was impressed with me too. It is too easy to stay in your "stupid place" because you don't want to admit to the idiocy of it. You actually lose more face that way, friends. I'm proud of me for pulling myself out of that.

I'd really like you to have that pride also.

Feel Empty Inside?

It is painful to hear so many callers who feel empty inside in spite of obvious blessings in their lives and the good things they do. One such caller, JoAnn, called to tell me that she had a perfect life with a good husband, four beautiful children, volunteer work, and the ability to stay home and raise her children and take care of the home.

I know that a 1960s feminista would already have the answer: "Go to work to get the sense of purpose and power that you'll never feel with home, hearth, and children!" Ugh. Obviously, I took a different tack to determine what JoAnn thought was missing from her life and making her feel so sad.

Dr. Laura: Give me a hint: what do you think is missing?

JoAnn: Well, let me tell you this, I've always felt like there was something missing. So I try to fill it with other things like getting involved in my kids' school and volunteering for this and that. I want to decorate my house and I want it to look this certain way and then I start to think none of it's really gonna matter for very much longer. So why am I gonna waste my money on material things right now?

Dr. Laura: I'm sorry, but I don't understand. If we have a birthday cake and we put candles on it, the person makes a wish and blows out the candles, then everybody's going to applaud and we throw the candles away. Does that mean we shouldn't have bothered to put candles on the cake?

JoAnn: No.

Dr. Laura: No? But that's what you're telling me—nothing matters because everything is transient. Well, you're right— that's life; life is transient. And as a matter of fact, I think that in human endeavors things have meaning especially because they are transient. Like when people say, "Enjoy your children because soon they'll be up and out; too tall and obnoxious, thinking they know everything at twenty," right?

Realizing that this was obvious and therefore probably not the issue central to her sadness, I asked her, "Who robbed you of your joy of being alive?"

She paused and then said, "I guess probably my dad. He was very angry and I was a pretty stupid kid and he reminds me of that."

At this point in our conversation I reflected on the tone she'd had since we began talking. Her tone was muted, seemingly calm—almost without the affect that should go along with her frustration. She was clearly a person who made good choices and who led a quality life with good behavior. She was also a person who wouldn't permit herself to reap the emotional rewards for her labors. That led me to:

Dr. Laura: I'm going to say something that sounds awful, but just work with me. Okay?

JoAnn: Okay.

Dr. Laura: Can you allow yourself to say you hate your father?

JoAnn: Um, not out loud.

Dr. Laura: Ohhhh. You don't have to mean it, you can take it back, but just say it.

JoAnn: (sigh)

Dr. Laura: Just say it.

JoAnn: (breath) I hate my father.

Dr. Laura: One more time—with passion.

JoAnn: I hate my father!

Dr. Laura: And that's true, isn't it?

JoAnn: (sigh)

It was at this point that I suggested that she's a good girl and good girls cannot possibly say such a thing. She feels sooo bad about herself for having those feelings that she really won't allow herself to enjoy life; that's her punishment for being a bad girl. Instead of sending JoAnn to her room without supper for having such evil thoughts, we're just not going to let her have pleasure in life.

> *Dr. Laura:* Any of that sound familiar?
>
> *JoAnn:* Yeah.
>
> *Dr. Laura:* So you see yourself as inherently a bad person who has a perfect life and doesn't deserve it, isn't that right?
>
> *JoAnn:* I don't feel like I deserve it.
>
> *Dr. Laura:* That's right, because you're bad and you know how I know you're bad? Your dad said so, didn't he?
>
> *JoAnn:* Yeah.
>
> *Dr. Laura:* So you're bad 'cause he said so and we know he's right. Wait a minute—how do we know he's right?
>
> *JoAnn:* (sigh) Because he's dad! That's exactly correct.
>
> *Dr. Laura:* So your husband who adores you and sees you as wonderful is a very stupid man because he perceives you as a good and terrific woman . . . one day he's going to find out he's wrong?
>
> *JoAnn:* (laughing)
>
> *Dr. Laura:* Don't you see, JoAnn, that the way you've lived

your life shows me and everyone else that your father is wrong?

JoAnn: (silence)

Dr. Laura: Now the gift I want to give you is to put yourself into that sentence: how JoAnn has lived her life ought to show JoAnn her father is wrong. That's the gift I want to give you. Are you going to accept it or are you going to be snotty and give it back to me?

JoAnn: (laughing) I'll take it. And thank you.

Dr. Laura: I want to ask you a question you might not be able to answer right now: do you feel empty right now?

JoAnn: No.

Dr. Laura: Okay.

JoAnn: (sigh)

Dr. Laura: I guess you filled yourself up with the truth of you.

JoAnn: (laughing) I will definitely work on it. Thank you very much.

Note: I did not ask her to confront her dad and tell him or anyone else that she hated him. That would have been nasty and destructive as well as not leaving her feeling less empty inside; in fact, the negativity from that interaction would have made her feel more empty because it would not have resulted in any positive action on her part.

She did have to admit to her rage at him instead of turning it into disdain for herself for having that appropriate rage. Did she buy her father's ugly perspective of her worth? Yes, but only in part. JoAnn knew she was kind, giving, and loving—but that image was counter to what she was still hearing from the sacred father image. More important, she'd never dismissed his evaluation in her own mind and heart, nor could she stomach the ugly feelings she had for him.

In those brief moments on the air, she got validation from me of what she knew of herself, and I gave her permission to send her dad to his room and accept the view of those who love her.

Hiding from Happiness . . . Just in Case

While JoAnn wouldn't allow herself to feel filled up with the joys in her life, joys that were the result of her own healthy efforts and quality existence, other people make sure they don't even get to have the joys. Why? Because they are, unfortunately, willing to be sad now and forever rather than be sad later—after tasting the wine.

Jane called my radio program to tell me that she's been shacking up with a guy for a dozen years in a nonsexual relationship and he won't marry her or leave. Essentially he first moved in as a roommate, but some three months into the relationship they started dating but never had sex.

She then threw in that she had wanted to get married and have children.

I told her, "No, you didn't. You really wanted to avoid it."

She came back with, "Really? Interesting."

Wow! How intellectual a response, I thought. I then proceeded to push her about three times to tell me why she would wish to avoid love, marriage, and family. Each time she'd come back with, "I don't know." I kept pushing. Finally she offered that her mother's death had hit her hard and her father was an alcoholic. She said she feared having a kid who would be an alcoholic.

It wasn't a difficult leap from there to an understanding of why she would waste a dozen years of her life in this unusual situation. It wasn't about a child becoming an alcoholic. It was about having one fear after another about loss and hurt, basically making her very avoidant of any kind of vulnerability.

Jane: Right.

Dr. Laura: Whining about him not ever following through is a red herring—this story plotline is about Jane avoiding re-creating the misery of her bio-family; so instead you created a different kind of misery.

Jane: I guess my question for myself is, you know, how did I let something like this go on for twelve years?

Dr. Laura: You wanted to avoid the things that would scare you about closeness and love . . . things you didn't experience as a child . . . things you didn't know how to handle and didn't want to risk.

Jane: Okay, Dr. Laura. You're right on.

Dr. Laura: Maybe now you're ready. Maybe that's why whining about his not marrying you is over and you're trying to get him out of your home. Maybe now you're willing to experiment with life.

Jane represents a lot of you who are terribly determined to avoid risk. You stay with the pain you know and avoid the possibility of joys, for the pains they might bring with them. You whine about your predicament and unhappiness, but choose that predicament and unhappiness over throwing your preoccupation with caution to the wind. Life becomes even shorter when you don't fill it.

Separate Reasonable Negative Emotions from the Rest of Your Life

Some of you consider yourselves one-note musical instruments: you're either happy or sad; angry or glad; hateful or loving; and so forth. In truth, ambivalence is a normal part of the human being—and being able to cope with more than one note or chord is essential to a full and joyful life.

Brenda, fifty-six, called to complain about taking care of her mom, who is going through cancer treatments. She admitted that being with her mom has brought out so much anger in her. She was willing to say, "I really hate my mom."

Her father had used her as a porn model along with her mother. She and her mother would wear matching baby-doll outfits. This started when she was ten and lasted until she was seventeen and stopped coming home from school. Her mother never protected her. I have found in the thirty-two years of radio conversations that the rage usually goes toward the person who didn't protect instead of the person who perpetrated.

She called me wanting to know how to get over this hatred for her mother. It was eating her up and confusing the situation with her being helpful to her mother during the mother's cancer treatment. She thought that there was some magical age where one automatically forgives and lets go of the emotions of anger. She thought she should be over it by now, in spite of the fact that her mother never acknowledged her breach of maternal trust and never apologized.

I told her that her parents were scum but this didn't mean that she had to get her life off track or spend her days drowning her sorrows and memories in hard booze, or spend every moment growling.

Her next step was to start the denial—and that amounts to self-denial.

Brenda: Maybe I'm making too much of this. Maybe I wasn't sexually abused.

Dr. Laura: Using children for sexual exploitation is a kind of rape; it is definitely abusive and sick.

Brenda: I just thought that I should stop that thinking at my age.

Dr. Laura: But she is scum. So are you going to say, "Blue is not blue, because at this age it shouldn't be blue anymore"? Scum is scum. That's a fact and facts don't change because you've had a birthday.

Brenda: Sometimes I think I make too much of it.

Dr. Laura: It's important to acknowledge the fact that there is evil and to hate it—that's healthy. I realize that acknowledging two scummy parents makes you an emotional orphan and you're somewhat loath to do that because it's an endpoint. So let me tell you this. You don't have to like her or forgive her to show compassion for her as a dying person. That tells me the quality of your soul—not the quality of her character; we already know that is low.

Brenda: Okay. That makes me kind of feel better and understand why I'm feeling this way.

Begrudging yourself your truth, the facts, makes you sad and keeps you whining. You can more productively function in life if you admit to the ugly truths and then decide—make a conscious choice—how to handle it. Again, confronting the evildoers is rarely satisfying and generally doesn't change them at all.

You have to decide your path through or around the ugliness to get to the beauty that is available in life: in quality relationships and loving acts.

Blessings Don't Obliterate Curses

It is important for me to reiterate that you need to understand that when people try to cheer you up by mentioning your blessings, they aren't trying to obliterate the reality of your pain and sadness (well, maybe some people are—but with good intentions); they are simply trying to give you a rope to grab onto so the ferocious current of pain won't sweep you away forever.

Laura wrote in response to hearing me talk to two women about their sadness:

"Like those two callers, I have always felt, 'How dare I feel sad when I have such a beautiful life?' But I DO feel that way, that I truly am appreciative of what I do have; a beautiful husband who has loved me since I was eighteen (I am now forty), an amazingly beautiful little miracle daughter (after tubal pregnancies) who is the light of our lives. But there are times that I want answers as to why my mom had to die so young with breast cancer and a stroke, why I had to lose four babies, why I cannot have any more children . . . and then I feel guilty for feeling that way.

"But after listening to your answers to both of those women callers, I realize that you can be appreciative for the blessings that you have and still feel sad about the losses in your life. They are not mutually exclusive feelings. The feelings can work together and both can help heal the hurts inside. Your answer to both of them spoke to me and I am vowing to move on, let the sadness and disappointments be, and enjoy the good that I have."

Whining is not a bad thing. Salt in soup is not a bad thing unless you overdo it. A certain amount of whining acknowledges the truth of the attacks on your well-being and very life. Whining lets you get out some negative energy, like frustration, in a non-cataclysmic manner. Whining basically presses the pause button and gives you time to think things through before you come up with a plan of action. Lastly, whining is an invitation for loving, caring friends and relatives to comfort you while you lick some wounds.

Whining is a bad thing only when you overdo it, marinate in it, and make it the only dinner course.

So whine for a while (I usually reserve a day and a half) and then get a plan. Margaret sent me a letter that may give you an example of what you need to do for yourself:

"The hardest step was writing out my resentments, then figuring out MY PART in them. This was the life-changing step that really gave me a new lease on life. No more self-pity. I check my motives in everything I do. I no longer play the victim and deal with life on life's terms. Also, the one day at a time rule helps, as when the past resentments are dealt with, we live in the present, we create instead of react to situations."

That's the key: owning your own attitudes, decisions, reactions, behaviors, choices, and emotional investment in the negative. Check yourself along the way each and every day. Challenge your reactions; redirect your energies. Take control. Become the master, not the slave of situations and your weaker, less constructive emotions. Make lists, celebrate your successes, and learn from your slipups.

Closing Sentiment

Maggie wrote explaining why she doesn't whine anymore. She recited three major things that remind her every day that her state of mind, mood, and preoccupations are up to her.

First, her sister was struggling with progressive multiple sclerosis (MS) for fifteen years. She was unable to move her body and now she had trouble speaking because of a loss of diaphragm control. Yet despite the constant readjustments she had to make because of each new loss, she enjoyed the most precious things in her life: her loving husband and devoted children.

"Everyone who knows her is drawn to her because she is a wonderful listener and nurturer. She has her moments of frustration and despair, but she told me, 'I have a choice. No one could criticize me for being sad all the time, but I choose to be happy, it's the one thing I do have control over.'"

Second, Maggie was impressed with her sister's husband. She described him as a man who had been transformed by his love for his wife, never focusing on what his wife couldn't do. No matter how much physical care he gave her, he always made it seem inconsequential. She remained his beautiful, supportive wife and safe haven. He depended on her calm strength and quiet wisdom and he expressed that feeling to their children. He regularly told them, *"I love your mother more with each passing day. She is the strongest, most beautiful person I have ever known."* It was therefore not surprising that they were thoughtful children who valued loving relationships and understood the profound joy that fulfilling an obligation can bring.

Third, Maggie had taught English to adult refugees from Bosnia, Sudan, and Iraq, as well as other hot spots for the past ten years. She recognized that these folks have physical and psychological scars that were beyond her comprehension. Sometimes these students would share something about their past that stopped her dead in her everyday tracks, and she was humbled and awestruck at the magnificence of the human spirit:

"That thing in people that makes them steadfast in their pursuit of a normal life; one in which they can hold on to family, friends, routine, work, meaning, joy, the things we Americans take so much for granted.

"My conclusion: it is so easy to be happy here in the United States. Everything in our lives, from simply getting out of a chair, walking, going to work, sending our children to school, talking politics, worshipping or not—all of these privileges must be cherished and guarded.

"My sister, her husband, and my students have taught me this. There are times when I feel like whining and I do. There are times when I feel irrationally sad, afraid, or hopeless. I guess that is part of being human. But I hold on to the image of these people and it helps me sort things out and focus on the bounty that is my life."

Amen.

CHAPTER 5

This Relationship Stinks

"Our life has gone from arguing, whining, rehashing, complaining and suffering to a more enduring life together by understanding each other's needs.

"Many of our pitfalls consisted of constantly fighting over who was right; much questioning about why this and why that. Just much selfishness from both our parts and having the 'getting back at you' attitude—all which led to discussions of divorce and how neither of us could deal with the other any longer.

"After we read The Proper Care and Feeding of Marriage, our life as a newly married couple was turned upside down. We could not believe how simple loving and being loved really is. We made a commitment, and that was to cherish and love one another for the rest of our lives. This is our goal."

—MR. AND MRS. ANONYMOUS, LISTENERS

M ore and more I get calls from newly married people, folks who couldn't wait to be together, who almost immediately are unbelievably ticked off with one another and are considering getting out. What happened to that honeymoon period before the seven-year itch? Who is teaching people how to actually *be* spouses?

I distilled *The Proper Care and Feeding of Marriage* into three essential (you heard me . . . essential!) points, after my first admonition of "choose wisely and treat kindly":

1. Treat your spouse as if you loved him or her with your last breath—no matter how contrary to that you might feel at any one moment.

2. Think hard every day about how you can make your spouse's life worth living.

3. Be the kind of person you would want to love, hug, come home to, and sacrifice for.

Instead, married folks these days seem to lean toward *not* seeing themselves *first* as a "married *couple*"—but seeing themselves as "married *individuals*" who can always find things to be ticked off about with their counterpart.

Sometimes people even wait until after the wedding to start complaining about things that occurred while they were dating but never discussed, or even more astonishing, they start developing hurt feelings about things the other experienced before they met! It's as though the marriage license was a license to gripe and whine instead of an invitation to love and be loved. Trust me, these days this behavior is just about epidemic.

And when this continues . . . marriages end even if the legal divorce is postponed until children are up and out. In fact, I took a call not long ago from a thirty-four-year-old woman married eighteen years (yes, the math is right) who didn't love her husband anymore and wanted to divorce. Their three children are fourteen, sixteen, and eighteen. I told her she had four years to go before divorce proceedings, because her kids needed the security and consistency of one home and not the chaos of divorce, enmity, visitation, and new "lovers." She was quite offended that her feelings were not paramount. I told her she had a moral obligation to the children to do whatever it took to make a kind atmosphere in the home.

Julie: But we aren't like that. We don't get along at all.

Dr. Laura: You have a moral obligation to behave sweetly,

nicely, and kindly to create a positive atmosphere for the three children. It matters for their future.

Julie: Oh please. I don't care to do that at all.

Dr. Laura: Do it anyway. Unilaterally, start being nice to him in private and in front of your kids. Just be nice no matter what. It's going to be good for your digestion and point of view about life in general and your life in specific. And you might be surprised at what comes from it: imagine being nice, that takes the edge off him and he's nicer, that takes the edge off you and you feel more comfortable . . . and so it might go.

I don't know if Julie followed my recommendation, but I'm sure lots of listeners took heed. It is very sad to me to keep receiving letters of regret from both men and women who did not follow my simple—and it is simple!—advice on being nice. The latest one is from Mary:

"Can you stand another letter about regrets? Well, here is mine. I am sitting here at three o'clock in the morning typing you because I feel if I can save one person from making all the dumb mistakes I did it will be worth it. My kids are on vacation with their dad and I won't see them for nine days and the reason I'm not with them is my fault and mine alone.

"I used to listen to you while I was married and always agreed with almost everything you said. I tried your books, your ideas, anything you had to offer, but I only tried it until I decided that I had tried long enough. I just decided my husband was different: that he was demanding and mean, that he would never change. I was

not going to waste my life on somebody who would not meet all my emotional needs.

"Well, you guessed it, I whined, I griped, I complained, and then I fell emotionally in love with someone who was not available in any sense of the word. I would show my husband, I told myself. I would find someone better than him.

"And guess what, I am sitting in my house alone at three o'clock in the morning missing my kids and the life I used to have. It wasn't perfect, but it was my life.

"I once got a fortune cookie that said, 'Stop searching, happiness is right next to you.' How I wish I would have taken those words to heart. Please, Dr. Laura, keep telling the women who think their situation is different that it probably isn't. There is nothing better 'out there.' There are just a lot of other messed-up people who are desperate for someone to come along and rescue them. I would give anything to go back in time and change the decisions I made. If I could, I would be on vacation with my family for the next nine days and not sitting at the computer at three o'clock in the morning messaging you.

"P.S. The reason I can't listen to you anymore is because when I hear your advice, I know that if I would have just done what you've said and written, that I wouldn't be where I am today . . . and it hurts."

I just don't want any of you to blow up a perfectly reasonable situation because of its imperfections or frustrations. In fact, I've discovered through my recommendations to callers and their feedback that the simplest adjustments can make all the difference in the apparent quality of their lives and marriages. Stop overthinking situations, stop overanalyzing motivations, and stop ruminating and whining. What should you do instead? Here's a great example:

A forty-six-year-old woman with an eight-year second marriage called (her adult children are out of the home) complaining that her husband is very involved with his older sister and her caretaking for their mother with Alzheimer's. He gives the sister money from their account and from the estate. Evidently he comes home from his mother's home quite upset and behaving angrily.

She wanted to know if she should divorce him; that consideration came to the fore after "reading books and having therapy," no less. I told her that leaving or staying is her decision alone, but if she wanted to keep this marriage she had to realize that the *situation* would not change (until the mother-in-law's eventual passing), but that her *reactions* and *behaviors* could change and that would positively impact her marriage.

I suggested that she needed to accept that his sister's sacrifice to take care of their mother and their financial needs would persist. It also seemed clear that since he was not as involved in the caretaking as their sister was, he had some guilt. His ability to donate financially was important to relieve his guilt. The best thing she could do was to ignore these issues—and never bring up the issue of money. Never bring it up, argue, or give opinions about the money drain or the time he spends at his mother's house.

I added that when he came home from a difficult time with them (after, for example, hearing his sister complain and having to face the fact that his mother is not there to some extent), she should greet him with a hot bath waiting and a glass of wine or hot cocoa. She needed to show him *compassion*. It is less likely that he would be hostile when she was being solicitous.

. . .

Another recent caller was complaining that her husband came home from work every day and literally freaked out if any little thing was out of place or not pristine. It seems his mother was unbelievably compulsive about the home being utterly perfect, and now that he's married, he's picking up the gauntlet; well, not exactly—he's not doing the cleaning, just the complaining.

I told her that each and every time he made a face or a comment about something in the home she should go up to him, hug him, and say, "It is more important that this be a happy and loving home than a perfect one." I made her practice it about half a dozen times until I could tell that we got the rage out of her voice and delivery. I explained that his mother was more concerned about the way the house looked (probably owing to an anxiety disorder) than the well-being of the people in it. As this is the emotional vacuum he grew up in, it is what he is most familiar with.

Interestingly, the very next day after this call occurred, I received the following e-mail from "Robert," who recognized himself in the husband of the caller:

"I listened to you coaching the caller to 'say it like she meant it' [that it was more important that this be a happy and loving home than a perfect one] *and it didn't sink in until that 'aha' moment that I have been doing that very same thing when I go home after a day at work.*

"I think I am like that guy, having grown up in a home with a 'supermom' who somehow kept everything immaculate and perfect without a speck of dust visible with four kids in the house.

"I come home and complain about the awful-smelling poopy diapers in the trash can, or stepping on a squished raisin or three in my socks where the baby was eating, smelly dishes left in the sink or

anything else that would happen in a normal day in a house where a family that has kids lives.

"When your caller hit that moment where she was able to put it in her own voice to tell her husband what was more important, I heard the hurt and emotion in her voice and recognized what I had ignored hearing in my own wife's hurt responses to my insensitive and plain old mean behavior.

"I am sitting here in tears imagining what my wife must think about around my coming-home time on any day with a little mess in the house.

"I am planning where I can stop by on the way home to bring her some flowers and start to make a dent in the apologies I owe her at this point. I plan on telling my wife what you had your caller practice telling her husband and plan on making this all up to my wife."

I'm thrilled out of my mind just imagining how many other husbands listened to that call and had the same personal shock of recognition. I have a feeling—or hope—that a lot more guys went home that night with flowers or a card and an apologetic demeanor.

Another listener, Amanda, send me one of those Internet goodies called "We all need a tree." As the story goes, a plumber was hired to restore an old farmhouse, and after he had just finished a rough first day on the job, a flat tire made him lose an hour of work, his electric drill quit, and his ancient one-ton truck refused to start. His temporary employer drove him home as he sat in stony silence. When they got to his house, the plumber invited the employer in to meet his family. As they walked toward the front door, the plumber paused briefly at a small tree, touching the tips of the branches with both hands. When opening the door, he underwent an amazing transformation: his face creased into big smiles and he hugged his two small children and gave his wife a kiss.

When the plumber walked the employer back to her car they passed the tree and the employer's curiosity got the better of her. She asked him about the tree and why he touched it as he had.

"I know I can't help having troubles on the job, but one thing's for sure, those troubles don't belong in the house with my wife and children . . . so I just hang them up on the tree every night when I come home and ask God to take care of them. Then in the morning I pick them up again. Funny thing is"—he smiled— "when I come out in the morning to pick 'em up, there aren't nearly as many as I remember hanging up the night before."

It is up to both the husband and the wife to use loving compassion to help each other cope with stresses; and each spouse has responsibility to minimize the figurative mud they drag into their homes on their shoes.

When Worse Never Gets Better

Bob called my radio program to tell me that he is now forty-three, married twenty years to a woman he dearly loves. However, the last ten years have been a terrible struggle. In the last year and a half she's been diagnosed with systemic lupus and encephalitis, the first an autoimmune disorder and the other a viral infection in her brain. He believes it is possible that things could be terminal. Sadly, she's meaner than ever. He was three years from leaving—

waiting only for the fifteen-year-old to become eighteen. Now with her illness, "Do I dare walk away?" he asked.

Dr. Laura: Not without losing the complete respect of your children. I'll tell you something: one of the stories I put in one of my books was a letter that stopped me in my tracks. The woman wrote, "I listen to your program and you tell people to stay for the sake of the children. I want you to know what my dad did for us. My mother was a raging schizophrenic—and I mean raging, violent, mean, unpredictable, drug and alcohol abusive . . . she was just horrible.

"We thought, my brother and I, that it would be the smartest thing in the universe for my dad to dump her, find somebody else, and be happy. He never did, until the day she died. And because of that, the two of us learned about commitment. Consequently we have good marriages, stable and wonderful kids, and we are grateful for every day we have with our spouses." So, Bob, that's my story for you.

Bob: Okay, well, thank you so much for everything you do and I haven't gone anywhere this whole time and I won't go anywhere.

Dr. Laura: Thank you. And your children will remember until their dying day that their dad taught them about commitment at the price of his own happiness.

Bob: Thank you.

Dr. Laura: And you didn't realize how important you are?

They know what kind of woman she is—and they know what kind of husband you are.

Bob: (crying) Thank you very much.

Dr. Laura: You're welcome, Bob.

Being "happy" doesn't just have to mean that you get what you want; a tremendous amount of happiness comes from the sacrifices you make to fulfill the needs of others who depend upon you.

Admissions and Humility

"I was an expert at cold wars," wrote Kimberlee.

"If my husband didn't do something I thought he would (came home too late or, God forbid, he should hurt my feelings), I'd completely shut down. Sometimes it lasted for days!

"After about twelve years into our marriage, we had been going through an especially trying time having begun our own business and learning to work together. This time, instead of fighting me, he described to me how he felt after a week or so of my coldhearted treatment. He choked up as he described the sadness, loneliness, and despair.

"It scared me to death! I thought he almost sounded suicidal. I had no idea how much my 'payback' was really killing him inside emotionally. It wasn't my goal to destroy him—I just wanted to be mad! I'm so thankful my husband told me the truth, and that I listened! I don't wage cold wars anymore. We just talk it out like

adults. We're celebrating—and I mean celebrating!—eighteen years now."

The single most powerful tool you have to make your life, with all its intimate relationships, a blessing is the willingness to look in the mirror and ask, "Mirror, mirror on the wall—tell me where I'm lacking, that's all." The mirror will be honest, and then you have the GPS route plotted out for you.

Allison wrote about spending most of her life as a big whiner and complainer. She learned from watching her mother that if you whine enough you get your way with your husband. She related whining to him about each and every dumb little thing with great regularity.

Her husband became that magic mirror. Instead of cowering, as her dad had done, he was, in her words, "a real man," and said—simply—"This behavior is not okay."

That's it! That's all! Mirrors tend to get right to the point.

At first she was stunned and upset. But willing to be introspective, she realized that she acted that way out of habit and selfishness.

Every now and then she catches herself whining and a disappointed look on her husband's face reminds her that she's not yet one hundred percent out of that habit.

It takes a lot of humility to use those moments as a catalyst for change instead of getting defensive, hostile, or catty. Humility is a hard pill to swallow—but it is worth it when, as Allison wrote, "my husband tells me he loves who I have become. I'm a lot happier with the new me too!"

Whining drags you down, simple as that. Whiners, while they get might their way or win some point, are still never truly happy. Why not? Because you've got to look for the next thing to be miserable about, and because you know you got what you manipulated and not what was given freely, and because you know that the other person is not adoring you. What is there to be happy about?

The whining behavior is not all about simple selfish manipulation. The last handful of decades have warped the delicate respectful and loving balance between men and women and morphed it into a war of rights without responsibilities. Balance is the important concept.

Louise discovered that:

"The first year of marriage was difficult because I made it so. I was always concerned that 'my rights' were being trespassed upon or that he was not allowing me my freedoms in some petty way.

"One day he told me straight out that it was important that I allow him to do the 'manly' chores of the house (fix the plumbing, take out the trash, etc.) and not always try to intervene to prove I was equally capable. He said he knew I was smart and quite able to do things, but it was important for his self-esteem as a man to take charge and to care for me.

"This was the turning point for me. I suddenly realized how much my trying to be his 'equal' was undermining his manhood. Sign me: a reformed feminist."

To some of you this latter admission may seem trivial. Believe me when I tell you it isn't. The feminista mentality is of female superiority and goes beyond legal considerations of equality; it virtually strips men of purpose and position and provides only a raw competition for power in the family. Love doesn't mean never having to say you're sorry; love means never making the other person sorry he chose you!

It is not only the feminist mentality that puts spouses on opposite ends of the sparring ring from one another; childhood dramas also play a large part. Amy called me a second time after I gave her an assignment at the end of our first conversation.

Amy: I originally called because I wanted to know how to stop my selfish behavior. But you pointed out that it wasn't an issue of selfishness toward my husband, but an issue of power and manipulation because I was protecting myself from my father—past history—while interacting with my husband—current history.

You asked me to treat my husband as though I felt safe with him and then call you back. I thought about the past and present and came up with ways I could do that.

Dr. Laura: Terrific—let me hear the list.

Amy: The first one is that in arguments and discussions I will not automatically defend myself because I'm safe—my husband is not out to get me. It doesn't make him happy when I make mistakes. I don't have to be perfect or always right.

Dr. Laura: He won't hurt you with it like your dad hurt you.

Amy: Yeah, yeah. My dad would make this big thing out of us being wrong. My husband doesn't do that, because he's really understanding. He wants me to just, you know, admit it and get on with life. It doesn't have to be a big thing. It's just about being honest.

Dr. Laura: And the next thing on your list?

Amy: The next thing is being completely honest and transparent and not trying to hide things—not trying to conceal things just so I will look better. I did that because I was afraid that if he sees the bad in me he won't love me. Like my dad, I worried that he only loves me when I'm good and perfect. But that is not why he loves me and that's not why we have a marriage.

Dr. Laura: The next thing on your list?

Amy: The next thing is that I would do and say things that reflect our *unity* and *interdependence*. I would do and say things behind his back to people just to show myself to be a strong woman. . . .

Dr. Laura: One whose father couldn't dominate.

Amy: Yeah, yeah—that's exactly true. The last one is that I would accept full responsibility for my mistakes. I realized how often I blame him just because I don't want everything that I've done wrong to be pointed out and I just put all of that on him. No more cop-outs. I'm just going to say, "I screwed up," and make it better.

Dr. Laura: And, unlike your father, your husband just lets it go.

Amy: Yes, he does.

To summarize, in Amy's mind she married her father . . . and she was not going to let her childhood happen again. However, the healthy part of her married a really good man. The haunted part of her led her to behave as though she hadn't; she didn't trust her own good choice.

I see this dichotomy quite often in callers. While it is true that many people marry exactly what they're running away from (a drunken, abusive, or neglectful parent), so many more marry just the right kind of person, but they fight the old war against the enemy with the very person who is their best ally. It is sad how many perfectly good relationships are destroyed this way. The unfortunate result is often the "ally" turning elsewhere for support, caring, appreciation, and affection. It is too easy to jump on allies for doing that. It is much smarter to look at why they're doing that.

Kim was smart:

"My own stubbornness almost cost me my marriage. Eight years ago I met and married a wonderful man. He is everything I ever wanted and yet I could not treat him right. I was always right, always doing more around the house—always better than him. This would have probably continued but for one fateful look at his cell phone.

"I had noticed that he had begun to withdraw, seemed less interested in me, and was starting to talk to me in a very angry way. We started sleeping apart, watching TV apart, and spending more time at work.

"To think I actually thought I could bully him into being nice to me. I screamed, was vindictive, and sometimes downright mean as I was demanding he love me.

"I saw a text message on his cell phone from another woman. When I confronted him he said that I was mean and that he did not want to be around me anymore. He said their relationship was not

physical, but the fact that he had to turn to someone else emotionally should tell me something. He said he loved me but did not think he could do it anymore.

"As my world crashed down around me, he told me he was leaving. We spent a long night talking—mostly me listening. We ended the night with the sweet man telling me that he would give me one more chance.

"I mustered all of your teaching and for the next week reached out to him, complimented him, and told him that I loved him. We had great sex every night. What resulted was him telling me that it was the best week of our marriage.

"I went right out and bought your two books on The Proper Care and Feeding of Husbands/Marriage. *It is now a month later, and although it has not been easy (I have some insecurities about the lady at work), I have come to the conclusion that if I take care of my husband and love him the way he deserves he will have no reason to confide in anyone else. That is what I can control—my actions and my words."*

I can't count the number of times a husband or wife has called me, his or her spouse having one foot in a divorce attorney's office or someone else's bed—and the other on a banana peel! If these callers are willing to admit, with humility, to their destructive behaviors without equivocation or blaming, I remind them that they hold all the cards.

1. There is a shared history that is touching and difficult to let go of.

2. There are children, pets, and projects in common that would be sad to only visit.

3. There are the memories of the good times.

4. There is the difficulty in making huge changes.

5. There are webs of family and friends to be considered.

6. There is the unknown.

That's but a brief list of what is on your side! All you have to do is become the kind of person and spouse your partner couldn't bear to be without. Threats, martyred behavior, attacks of the vapors, laying guilt . . . none of these have the power of humility and love.

The Revelation Moment

I've been deeply gratified with the number of letters I've been receiving since *The Proper Care and Feeding of Husbands* and *Marriage* were published—especially when the writers expressed having an "aha!" moment of revelation, as I call it, that completely redirected their response to a typically potentially disastrous moment. Keep in mind that these situations are generally seen, when described to friends or relatives, as moments of justifiable rage. Nonetheless, the folks who listen carefully to my program and writings get the subtle but powerful point that there is probably another, equally powerful way to look at the problem.

Here's one example: A woman, seven months pregnant—with the discomforts that often come from this delicate condition—wrote about an incident with her husband. He had come home late from working hard. It would seem he was hoping for some romantic intimacy (aka sex) when she said, "I don't feel particularly well," and he proceeded to go downstairs, make himself something to eat, and watch TV. She stayed in bed crying, feeling sorry for herself and really quite angry with her "insensitive" husband.

Hours later he came to bed. At some point in the night, she awoke to find him massaging her back and shoulders. Evidently doing so was not typical for him, so she felt twice as pleased. Then he said, "I have been working late so much and I have been missing you. I love you so much." She noticed that he was getting aroused.

Her first reaction to his arousal was anger: "Oh, I get it, he is just trying to get some action—he isn't just comforting me." Her anger increased as she thought about how he knows she hates getting awakened, especially because her pregnancy was making it difficult for her to sleep.

Then: THE DR. LAURA REVELATION MOMENT!

"I could hear you saying something to the effect of 'Geez, woman, here is the man who is working his butt off to provide for you; who can look at his woman in her HUGE pregnant state and tell her that she is HOT and tell her that he loves her and misses her when he is away, and you have the NERVE to be pissed because, heaven forbid, he wants to make love to his wife. I feel sorry for HIM!'

"I laughed to myself as I realized this great man was showing me in his way that he loved me and cared for me and was sorry that I was struggling and wanted me to know that he thought I was hot and sexy. I didn't want anyone to feel sorry for my husband because of me. I want them to be jealous of his hot pregnant wife.

"So I kicked those negative thoughts to the curb, turned to my husband and said, 'You are so hot, babe. I love you too!'

"It made for a FABULOUS night, great sleep, and good feelings this morning. Thank you!"

Now don't you find it amazing that a woman, laden with baby, feeling tired and put upon, could switch into sex kitten just with the revelation that doing so was a great thing and not an imposition?! It just goes to show you that our physical state of being is sometimes tragically impacted by a negative state of mind. However, that state of mind is readily morphed into a positive one once you're willing to see the irony in the revelation. In a blink, she went from "man, the insensitive sex maniac" to "man, the incredibly sensitive lover."

Another typical complaint that requires the revelation moment or a marriage becomes combustible is this issue of time spent alone. Many women, at-home moms in particular, call to complain that their man is struggling with school—to get ahead in a profession that will take better care of them—and work—so that they can keep a roof over their heads and food in their tummies—and has left them pretty much holding the bag at home.

The first obvious observation is: In your next life, plan to marry and have children *after* your man has completed all the preparations for the nest. Birds don't usually make a home and lay eggs in a nest until it is complete. Doing otherwise makes life ever more difficult—not impossible, just doable.

The second obvious observation is the revelation! Jennifer had it listening to me taking such a phone call:

"As difficult as our circumstances are for me sometimes, since I am obviously on my own much of the time and we have to live a very frugal life, your caller reminded me of how lucky I am with my husband. He does what he does for me/us and he NEVER complained about how tired HE must be since most nights he gets less than five hours of sleep on top of putting in these incredible

hours. He simply does what needs to be done because he IS a MAN who has stepped up the plate to still provide for his family while trying to set his family up for a better life once he is done with school.

"We see the light at the end of the three-year-long tunnel regarding school as he has only about nine months left now. We look forward to seeing him more, but in the meantime, your caller has reminded me of the incredible value in my man who I intend to outwardly appreciate much more than I often do—and to stop complaining about the long hours I am left with as a result of his absence. I SHOULD just be thankful for his absence as that allows me to be my kids' mom . . . times four!"

There you have it. The "facts" aren't changed. But the revelation moment will help you see that you are actually benefiting at the time you can only see yourself suffering or losing. One woman called to complain that her husband was gone two nights a week for business (she didn't suspect any fooling around) and she was home with the three small children. She was sniffling and whining on the phone. I tried to be helpful, as usual, but frankly, I lost patience with this woman because she just wouldn't accept any other view of her situation. I told her that while she was in her own bed, doing whatever she chose and in whatever order each day, eating when and what she pleased, playing with and enjoying her children, and so forth, her husband didn't have his own bed nor the comfort of his own woman and children at the end of a long day.

Hopefully, she had the revelation moment after we finished the call.

Sex Has Powers . . .

I'm sure I've stunned some new listeners when they hear the advice I give to a seemingly wide range of marital issues to "have a good night tonight seducing the heck out of him/her with great fun and passion!"

Most people tend to look at sex as something you do only when you are in the best of moods and your spouse has been appropriately obedient, or it's ovulation time and you want to conceive. I have no issue with the latter, but the former is truly backward. Sex heals many wounds, eradicates a particularly bad mood or memories of an unfortunate day, releases tensions and exasperations, brings a couple closer, forgives trivialities, and generally brings a great mutual smile to the marriage.

In other words: sex first usually leads to less bitching and bad feeling later!

NEVER use a lack of sex to punish, make a point, hurt, frustrate, or otherwise.

Cathy heard me talking to some female callers who were not having sex with their husbands because they thought their own bodies were ugly. Funny, men never call me with that concern about their own bodies. Anyway, I've told women that they should ask their husbands if they'd prefer their wives to be perfect, or naked and up close and personal.

Cathy wrote:

"Any time I start looking in the mirror and criticize my saggy this or lumpy that, my husband just stares at me and says, 'You better not ever talk about my beautiful wife like that again!' That

always shows me just how beautiful I am to him—just as he is to me."

I just love when listeners prove my point! Men may look at "ten" girls who walk by, but a woman who treats them right and loves them up is always a "ten" to them, no matter what the sags and bags may be.

However, the more important issue about sex is its remarkable healing properties.

"Smiling again in Costa Mesa," is how one woman signed her e-mail to me with the following story. She and her husband had been married for twelve years and had two boys and ran two businesses together. Most of the time she reported that they managed very well, but one particular Wednesday he blew up at her over something she thought was minor. He was so aggravated and frustrated (probably overwhelmed and on the fast lane to burnout) that he didn't have much to say to her for two days! She was very upset by it, of course. She figured, after spending some years listening to my program, that just talking about it wasn't going to cut it—he had to actually see changes in her, not just hear about them.

One evening he was just tossing and turning in bed, obviously not able to get comfortable and fall asleep.

"I lay there listening to you (Dr. Laura) in my head saying, 'Just go for it—he won't say no!' So praying you were right, I stripped off my clothes and cuddled up next to him and whispered, 'Let me do one thing I can do right. I'm not asking you to stop being mad—but I know I can help you sleep.'

"There was no response for about thirty seconds (which seemed like forever) and then he slowly rolled over with open arms. He thanked me and woke up this morning and made me breakfast."

Too many of you think you have to talk/yell/fight it out to resolve problems. Nah! All you have to do is show some humility and own up to your error even if, as in our last listener's letter, you don't happen to think it is a big deal and then turn on the soft or passionate affection to seal the deal. Great sex between spouses having some problems is like rebooting your computer. And yes, it does often solve the problem because when people feel more fun, close, and excited about each other, they generally behave better without having their inadequacies shoved up their noses.

And while I'm using the word "sex" to make my point, let's make sure we understand that there is plain sex (which you could have with a stranger at a bar) and making love (which you can have only with someone familiar to your heart). I made this distinction to a couple who called my program and it turned night into day almost immediately.

Kristy (the wife) and Chris called my program after being married for nine years and having three children (eight, six, and three). Kristy had been suffering with endometriosis with its pain and bleeding that made sex less appealing because of the discomfort. After a hysterectomy, she now felt like a different person—free and like a woman. Now that she could get back into the game, he seemed to have issues.

Chris had to get up early (6 A.M.) to be to work by 7 A.M., so he had to go to bed around ten, ten-thirty. Kristy stayed up later . . . so they never got any.

Kristy: That's not how I see it at all. I think that's just stupid and silly. I'm handled and touched and mommied and fondled by kids all day long and I need my time. And he's very particular about when he's ready to go to bed—and it is HIS time, y'know, when he wants it. And if I don't engage him at that exact time, then I'm a bitch, and I don't love him, and I'm rejecting him. Y'know—it just totally gets blown out of proportion.

Dr. Laura: Chris, is that how you experience this situation?

Chris: Except for the part that she thinks it is silly and stupid and no big deal. Well, it IS a big deal, because I can't stay up till twelve, one o'clock in the morning when I have to get up and be productive at work the next day.

Kristy: I went to bed with you at ten-thirty, Chris, and I went to sleep. Apparently I was a cold fish.

Well, before this escalated even more, I put a stop to their complaining. I told them that they were not talking about making love—they were talking about having sex. To further the distinction I made above, having sex is about getting pleasure when you feel like it. Making love is tending to the other person's need for tenderness, affection, and sexual release regardless of what you feel like.

Dr. Laura: Chris, imagine taking Kristy into the bathtub, rubbing her feet, and telling her to relax after a long day with three kidlets. She'd probably get turned on. I think this situation can be fixed if you two stop thinking about intimacy as sex and think about it as making love to the other person—because then you'll think about the other person's schedule, context, need for touching, affection, and sweetness—and I think this will all work out.

Your assignment—and call me next week—is to spend a week not having any sex—but just making love. So that means that instead of thinking "Am I getting any?" you're going to be thinking about how you're going to actually make love to the other.

They did call back in a week—and the results were exactly as I had predicted.

Dr. Laura: Welcome back. Your assignment was to not have sex, but to love each other and make love to each other for the week—and we've done that and it's been awesome! How did that shift your thinking or behavior?

Kristy: It made a big difference. Actually, just in shifting the mind-set in that direction. It made a big difference in our intimacy.

Chris: Yeah, me too. It seemed effortless. It was like she was on the same page as I was.

Kristy: We wanted each other. It was mutual.

What was particularly cute about these two is that my screener, Kimberly Neill, heard them saying "I love you, baby," and such to each other while they were getting ready to come on the air. Oh, what a difference a concept makes!

Respect Their Parenting Role

This subject could be a whole book! However, there is one most typical situation that deserves special notice here: assuming too much unilateral control over parenting for power or for popularity. No matter what the motivation, it is destructive to marriage, family, and child behavior.

The whining factor is a huge part of this problematic situation. One parent interferes with just about everything the other parent tries to do and still complains about being overburdened and having to correct everything the other parent does.

One listener, Rachel, got this message big-time.

"I am listening to a call from a woman whose adult son and her new husband (stepson/stepdad) have a conflict. You told her, 'Let the two of them talk directly to one another, and stay out of it. They will work it out—or not—but either way, you need to butt out!'

"I have heard you tell people over and over—that the only people 'in the middle' are those who wish to be there. I would love to share with you how you helped my family this time: My son was home from college for the summer and he and my husband were constantly butting heads, and for the life of me, I couldn't tell you who was right or wrong. And I was sick of each of them bringing it to ME, because I did not wish to be in the middle . . . or so I thought. One day, after yet another quarrel between them, I said to myself, 'What would Dr. Laura tell me to do?' 'Get out of the middle!'

"So I sat the two of them down and said, 'I love you both and it hurts me when you cannot get along. This house is too small for arguing. It is not fair to me that you should quarrel in the house and destroy my peace. Therefore I am packing a bag and moving out.

Call me when you work it out. Once I am gone, do not dare sit here pointing fingers at each other because both of you working together made my home so unpleasant that I no longer wish to be here. Both of you did this, not just one.

"I packed a bag and went to a hotel. I think they was in shock—I know I was. And I confess that as I drove away I was immediately anxious and worried, wondering if I did the right thing and if I should turn around and go back and try to 'referee' some more.

"I drove for several hours, checked into a hotel, and that night I got a call from my contrite family. Since I redirected the two of them back to one another, they get along much better—it could not, would not have happened unless I removed myself.

"I had some insight into the reason why a person might wish to be in the middle: it is gratifying and powerful because everyone likes you, gets along with you, and is currying your favor in order to manipulate you into picking their side. So I had to let that go in order to help them improve their relationship. It was worth it."

The Absolute Best Way to Fight!

I remember when I was in training for psychotherapy, how they would have us role-playing all sorts of interactions; fair fighting was my favorite. Why? There is no such thing. Fighting is always destructive. Some folks want to fight because they have deluded themselves into thinking that if they keep beating on a person or an issue the situation will become entirely different. For example, fighting about smoking when you married a smoker who promised to stop but he/she didn't and you went through the ceremony anyway and now spend precious time in life fighting over it daily. To these people I say, "Accept that he/she is a smoker and just ask him/her to do it outside. If it was so important to you, marriage should have been out of the question. But once you accept him/her—it is, as they say in women's clothing stores, as is." No whining!

Fighting as a tool to dominate or protect your own ego is equally destructive—and the act of domination and your ego are tightly intertwined. When you're afraid you won't look good to your spouse—which will make him or her stop loving you—and you attempt to remedy that by blaming the spouse for somehow causing you to make some mistake or push you to your own bad behavior, or beating the spouse up (figuratively) to even the "looking bad or stupid" score . . . what do you end up with? Easy! You end up not being loved because none of that is lovable behavior. Amazing and ironic, don't you think?

So how do you express concerns and hurt feelings, and hash out differences in desires or opinions about significant issues? First, make sure it is actually significant before you bother. I think we should, as a first approximation, give the win to the person who cares the most if the issue is really not that important to you. Hey, it isn't about wins and losses—it's about love till death do you in!

The biggest technique I'd suggest follows much of the advice I've given throughout the book: give, give, give, give, and give some more.

Jessica and Junior called my radio program. They'd been having lots of problems in their six-year marriage that had already produced three children.

Jessica: We've been arguing a lot lately. We don't know how to work our problems out. We need advice from you because the advice we're getting from our family isn't helping.

Dr. Laura: Junior, please give me an example of an argument.

Junior: A money situation one?

Dr. Laura: How could you make her feel better about the money situation?

Junior: I could come home and just give her all the money: the whole check.

Dr. Laura: You bring home the money and let her budget it and pay the bills?

Junior: Exactly, yeah.

Dr. Laura: And Jessica, how could you make Junior feel very good about the money situation?

Jessica: Talking with him over it?

Dr. Laura: No. That's mostly useless. You've talked a lot to him already. Think about something you could do to make him feel better about the money situation. Last chance!

Jessica: I don't know what to do.

Dr. Laura: I gave the hint—when you have a problem, instead of getting angry about how you feel and how the other is not accepting your point of view, think—think long and hard about how you can make the other feel better about the problem.

Marriages aren't happy because there are no problems. Marriages are happy because the spouses are a team, not just two brats who want their own way. I'm suggesting that you *not talk* about these issues. I'm suggesting you think inside your own heads and hearts: what can I do to make *him/her* feel better about the problem.

Fights are never geared toward an equitable conclusion. Fights are geared toward winning something for yourself. I love the technique that some parents use to teach their children about not fighting over resources—like pies. The key is to ask one child to cut the pie and then have the other child select who gets which piece. It's amazing how quickly they learn something about working together.

So here it is, simply put: when you have an issue that sparks tempers, make sure you both understand the parameters, then go off into your own corner and figure out how you can make your spouse happy about any conclusion.

I recently took a call from a woman who wondered if she had to invite her husband's widowed mother and alcoholic, divorced brother to her own mother's Thanksgiving dinner. It seems there is a history of his mother and brother behaving very badly. Her husband wants the invitation to be made, out of a sense of loyalty and guilt. And now they fight with whining on both sides.

The wife, of course, didn't want them anywhere near Thanksgiving dinner with her family, as it always gets ugly. I suggested she tell her husband, "Honey, why not have a special time with your mother and brother at our home on Thanksgiving eve?" This keeps her family's celebration calm, treats her husband's family well, and gets her husband off the hook. See? Simple! Just figure out how to make it good for the other person.

I Think We Should Get a Divorce!

Ouch! It is very ugly when arguments lead to threats of abandonment. One caller, Lindsey, wanted to know how to get her husband to stop making those threats, since he doesn't seem to ever mean it enough to follow through. I told her to stop talking and just look at him, just look up at him with her big baby blues. That's it. Say nothing. He will be the next one to speak. That will extinguish the behavior very quickly. But importantly, I wanted to know what is going on that is so severe and unpleasant that he keeps feeling like evaporating.

Lindsey: I'm not taking care of the finances like he would want them to be taken of. I'm not sticking within the budget of the groceries, clothes for our daughter . . . I guess we're living the same lifestyle as we were before I became an at-home mom. We had more money. And we need to tighten up our budget perhaps now.

Dr. Laura: Okay, well then . . .

Lindsey: I feel it's unrealistic what he is expecting.

Dr. Laura: Oh, come on, Lindsey. You have a lot less money. Since you're no longer earning an income, the burden is now on him and he's scared. He wants to please you and your skirting of financial responsibility makes him feel undermined and inadequate. This is so simple, there's no reason you should fight.

I frankly don't understand why people get married, love each other, make babies, and look at each other like the enemy, a hostile parent or a competitor.

Money is tight because you and he wanted to do the right thing as a family and raise your own children. He's freaked out and being insecure, because young men his age are not brought up to have pride in the fact they are supporting their family. So you need to say to him, "You're right. I have to work harder at budgeting. I'm sorry. And here's my plan."

Lindsey: I guess I know what the problem is. He wants to buy a home, and the money's not there.

Dr. Laura: Great. So say, "You know what? I want to buy that home too. I realize that we had to pick the house or raising our children ourselves—and we happily picked our kids; and I'm very grateful to you that you're on the same page as me as to what's most important. Someday we'll have a house." That's how you talk to your husband.

Lindsey: It's true. He's a good man. He's just trying to do what he can for the family. When he gets so mad, I just escalate it. I guess because I feel insecure.

Dr. Laura: Cut the "you're hurting my feelings," and take care of your man. The more you take care of his ego, the more he'll take care of you!

. . .

Like all the issues I've given examples of, it's about thinking him/her versus me, me, me. In a recent call, a woman married two years to a man with three children between ages twenty-two and twenty-six called to whine about their argument over trimming the tree. He wanted to wait until his children come (some five days before Christmas), while she wanted to do it in advance because she just wants to feel the holiday spirit longer.

I said, "My dear, your wish is for yourself, his wish is for his family. Based on that observation, what do you think is the right thing to do?"

Believe it or not, she said, "Do it the way I want because he and I are 'family.'" I came back with, "No, you are the new wife; he's had a family for thirty years that you're joining. Respect his family—his children and his bond with them—or keep whining and see how long he'll have wife number three!"

I realize that sounded tough, but sometimes it is tough to get through people's whiny selfishness.

Closing Sentiment

Abele wrote:

"Listening to your show yesterday and hearing the nagging, whining women talking about how bad they have it prompted me to send this to my husband this morning, so he would have it when he first walked into his office:

REMEMBER . . . I love you more than life

REMEMBER . . . You make me smile every day

REMEMBER . . . *That most people can only WISH to have
   what we have together*
REMEMBER . . . *That we chase our dreams together and
   CATCH them*
REMEMBER . . . *That little things like bills cannot hold us
   back!*
REMEMBER . . . *That we are NOT tied to anyone or
   anything EXCEPT for each other*
REMEMBER . . . *That we are still at the BEGINNING of
   our adventures!*
REMEMBER . . . *That I am TOTALLY in love with you*
Your admiring wife, Abele"

Wow! Now that's a lot better than whining.

CHAPTER 6

The Earth Is Not the Center of the Universe—and You and I Aren't Either!

"When I was first married, I was a whiner, talked incessantly and would never let go of an argument even when one didn't exist. After a pivotal argument with my husband, he took off his wedding ring and left in on the dresser and then went to bed. It was the defining moment. I was devastated.

"I realized I had been taking him for granted. He worked so hard, was so patient, such a good lover, friend, and dad, yet I thought I could treat him any way I chose and he'd still be there.

"I found a way to look outside of myself with a job and with volunteer work. I started working with troubled kids—kids that just needed me. Soon I learned how to listen to my husband and his needs—just listen. We still have our ups and downs, but the ups are far greater in number than the downs."

—LESLIE, A LISTENER

I remember a story my mother told me when I was a young girl about how none of us is the center of the universe. My mother was sixteen when her mother died of breast cancer. She was devastated. Looking out the window of her home one day soon after the death, she noticed that people were walking, bicycling, and driving; laughing, talking, and eating. She wondered how they could possibly just go on with their lives as though this tragedy to her had never happened! It stunned her into the recognition that each of our lives is circumscribed by our own feelings and experiences and that this is true for every person in the world.

This explains how easy it is to (1) drown in your own ego or pain and (2) discount the needs and feelings of others because of your own pain. Have you seen the television commercial from an insurance company that shows a woman at a corner grabbing the arm of a stranger as he almost steps into the street when a car is coming? Another watches that act of thoughtfulness and helps someone else while being observed by yet another stranger. This goes on until we get back to the original woman being impacted by viewing someone else in a good deed. This highlights one more important concept: we are ultimately dependent upon and impacting others in ways we don't even realize.

Think about it; you let somebody cut ahead of you in traffic, they are surprised and grateful, that reduces their stress and tweaks their positive energies so that when they reach home they give their kids and spouse a big hug with a smile. If you hadn't let them in with a kind wave, they might grouse all day and kick the dog before slamming through their front door.

So while there is a natural reaction to be consumed with what is in your head, don't underestimate your value to others as well as the impact of the consequences of your actions and choices. With that concept in mind, I'd like to tell you about a call with Jose that will probably make many of you feel as though I could be talking about you.

Jose called to tell me that he has an issue with his mom because she gave him a bad stepdad.

Jose: And sometimes when I'm driving, I'm thinking about my mom, and I feel like calling her and telling her that I love her and want to give her a kiss. But when I actually go to her house and I see her, I don't want to give her a kiss anymore for some reason, y'know. And my question is, why is that?

Dr. Laura: Because you're angry and the kiss would be a fake. You want to have a mom to kiss—but this one, yours, disappointed you so much you can't feel that warm. She hasn't apologized, has she?

Jose: No—we have had a lot of arguments about it.

Dr. Laura: She knows she did something wrong, but she doesn't want to admit to it. And that's a really stupid thing that people do, because if they would admit to it, they'd feel relief, the person they hurt would feel relief, there'd be a better atmosphere and more happiness all around.

Jose: Okay. And she gives me a kiss, and I feel like I don't want her kiss, but I do inside of me . . .

Dr. Laura: That's what I just explained: you want *a* mommy to kiss you—just not that one.

Now up to here you're probably wondering why I have added this conversation to this chapter on, basically, seeing outside of yourself. Well, friends, here it comes:

Jose: And I have another question—it's my kids. I love my kids, but sometimes, y'know I even feel that way with my kids. When they come close to me, I just feel like I don't want them close to me. But then I hug them and tell them that I love them—because I know that's right to do. But I still feel that inside of me . . . I don't want to.

So here is an example of what I mean by indicating that your choices, demeanor, and behaviors impact others—and for that you must accept responsibility and do the morally right thing for others, even if it starves you.

Fortunately, Jose is faking it with his kids because he is a good man and does for his children what he knows they need even though it causes him pain. Now the interesting question is why would it be difficult for him to give or receive loving affection from his children? You can understand his ambivalence with his mother: she betrayed him and didn't protect him and never admitted her wrongdoing.

But what about his children? Aren't they just innocent bystanders?

Dr. Laura: Jose, listen up and carefully. You're still trying to be a little boy . . . holding out for the time you'll be perfectly parented by a loving, caring mom. And right now you're jealous that your children get more love from you than you got from your mom and stepdad. You keep holding on to that hope that your mommy will turn into a good mommy. Give up the hope. Your mother is who she is. She knew you were being hurt. She didn't care—as long as she had somebody taking care of her.

Now, I don't mean you're not lovable, and it does not mean you don't deserve love. And it does not mean that you have no love inside of you.

When your kids come to you to be hugged, I believe that you're upset because you want to be the kid. *You* want to get the hug! But here's how I look at this: you did not have loving parents. And there are two ways you could look at this: (1) you can spend the rest of your life pouting, or (2) you can say God gave you two opportunities for a parent/child relationship. The first one—when you're a child—you have no choice about. The second one—as the parent—you have all the ability to make yourself the parent you wish you had.

So when your kids come up and want hugs, close your eyes, squeeze them, hug 'em, kiss 'em, tickle them . . . and try to feel what they are feeling from you. Stop being hungry but refusing to eat: let them fill you up with the love you missed. Let that love heal your hurts. Don't deny yourself that emotion anymore. Just because you had to live without it growing up doesn't mean you have to doom yourself to never being able to enjoy it.

Let your children's love heal you, Jose.

At this point, Jose was crying softly. That made me so very happy—because it meant that the barrier he put up, denying his need for love and therefore pushing away the fulfillment of that need, had probably come to an end. Remember, your pain isn't just yours, because how you handle that pain in your life impacts everyone around you who cares about you.

Lynn called my program to ask why she felt responsible for everything, which is bringing her a lot of anxiety. I explained to her immediately that the anxiety comes first, actually, and the symptom of that anxiety is an attempt to control whoever and whatever in order to alleviate the anxiety. Lynn understood that she's controlling, making sure everyone rises to a certain standard, for which she takes personal responsibility, because when she was a kid, "I was never good enough. And I want them all to be good enough."

Dr. Laura: So you don't want them to suffer like you did?

Lynn: I just want them all to be accepted in society . . . so they're accepted by people.

I then gave her an assignment: to close her eyes and imagine she's in the middle of the room, and all around her are mirrors. I gave her about four minutes during a newsbreak, and when we came back I asked her how it was.

Lynn: It was horrible. I don't want to look in the mirrors. I guess when I look in the mirrors, I am constantly finding something wrong with me.

Dr. Laura: You're doing great . . . keep going . . .

Lynn: Okay. I keep trying to find a place where I wouldn't have to face myself.

Dr. Laura: You don't want to face yourself, so you nag *others* into being perfect.

Lynn: You're right. And that causes the anxiety.

I went on to explain to her that her initial assumption of forty-six years was wrong and it was sad for her, and sad for the folks she's tormenting in her life. I told her she wasn't wrong, bad, stupid, ugly, or dumb . . . but that she was a pain in the butt to others because of her hatred of what she accepted from her parents as a correct assessment of her worth.

Of course, she wanted to know what the *quick* fix was. I told her there actually was one . . . sorta.

Dr. Laura: You have to accept that your original assumption that what your parents taught you about yourself is not true.

Lynn: Okay.

Dr. Laura: And here it is—the quick fix! Every time you feel yourself getting revved up to be controllingly bitchy, nagging, demanding, critical, judgmental, and pushy, just say out loud to yourself, "I AM OKAY. I am as okay as everybody else—a little better than some and a little worse than others—but basically okay." Enjoy your good points and qualities a bit more.

Whatever you're experiencing, it's impacting others—to whom you are obligated to be your best and healthiest self. It isn't just about your pain—it's the splash-out or ripple effect that can be benevolent or destructive that you have to take responsibility for.

Children Redirect Our Inherent Selfishness

Becoming a parent is quite probably the single most dramatic lesson in giving up looking at yourself as the center of the universe. It is amazing how something that small, that cannot walk, talk, scratch its nose, or feed himself or herself, rules the home and your life on a minute-to-minute basis! You can no longer decide on a moment's notice to do this or that, even shower, when you'd like, because the child's needs are relentless and important. Parenthood is the most serious foray into the philosophically elevated concept of living for someone or something outside of yourself.

For most of you, the responsibility of caretaking for a totally dependent human being is an even more dramatic challenge than marriage. When dealing with their spouse, another adult, people feel—too much so, I believe—free to manipulate, negotiate, or compete; none of that works with screams of hunger and dirty diapers.

I am not only addressing the time commitment, I want to bring more attention to the emotional qualities that have to be confronted within your own psyche. There is no reason that every insecure or unpleasant feeling you have must be expressed or respected. And when you have children, that reality becomes seriously clear.

Cynthia wrote about her lesson in selflessness and children:

"Having children did the most to change my destructive thoughts. Changing the center of my life from myself to someone else and making the conscious decision to create the type of home I wanted for my family were natural extensions of becoming a mother and wanting a happy home. Rehashing was 24/7 part of my life before because of all of my childhood physical and verbal abuse by my mother. I finally had to decide that she could not have any emotional control over me anymore. If I had to keep rehashing about how unfair my life had been, I was basically holding my own happiness hostage and not, as you've said on the radio program, going to get any final justice.

"I had to be an example to my children and I had an obligation to my children to be a happy person. While many of my relatives are hurtful, the triumph is that my family is loving!"

I ask many parents calling my program to complain about their lives, their childhood, their bad luck with whatever, and their gripes about family and neighbors. I always come back to the idea of making the house a home. A house is a place of residence. A home is a refuge that requires your influence to create its beauty, safety, peace, and loving. I have told some callers that when they want to throw a hissy fit about something they should actually walk outside the home to do it—preserving the sanctity of that home.

Obviously many emotional moments are spontaneous and can't really be put on hold for a walk around the block. Nonetheless, a cup of coffee, a hot bath, whistling, hugging, reading aloud, playing a board game . . . something to take your attention away from the monotony of your complaints about your life.

Just the other morning I got some really lousy, upsetting news. I frothed for about five minutes, went for a hike, did some yoga, hit some tennis balls, shot some pool, and had lunch. By the time I had to go on the air I was completely at peace with the "problem," realizing it will work itself out in its own way and my whining about it wasn't going to power that engine. I'm telling you this about myself because I don't want anyone to think I'm immune from needing and taking my own advice.

Remember, for the sake of your children, your home needs to be a sanctuary—even from your own inner demons.

Even Addictions Have Responsibility

I'm of the opinion that all irresistible impulses are simply impulses that haven't been resisted. I don't subscribe to alcoholism as a disease; it is a bad habit that has severe consequences for health, maturity, responsibilities, and relationships. People can make the choice to stop drinking, smoking, sniffing, Internet "porning" whenever they wish. That it might be difficult and uncomfortable is a given. That it will be accomplished with grit and support is also a given. Motivation is everything. Commitment to others is essential.

Kathie had been a heavy smoker her whole adult life. Someone had suggested she go to a hypnotherapist to help her break the serious addiction to nicotine. She followed through and was told by the hypnotherapist that she'd have twenty days of difficulty. She listened to tapes and did breathing and imagery assignments—but on the twenty-first day she freaked out completely because the urge to smoke was as large as ever. Her blood pressure and weight went sky-high. She gained over seventy-five pounds and got so depressed that she cut off her hair one night and left the scissors on the kitchen floor because she felt an urge to slit her wrists . . . but didn't really wish to die.

Nonetheless, she stayed off cigarettes for that year—dealing with chaotic emotions and weight issues. Her poor husband went on antidepressants to cope with all this turmoil.

"This was such a huge effort. I remember getting out of my car one day and feeling like, 'How can I go on like this. I hurt . . . argggggh.' I would stop and think, 'okay . . . feel my arms . . . legs . . . I feel horrible, but I'm still alive. My emotions may be trying to tell me how bad I feel, but when I really think about it, and stop to take count—I'm still here . . . I'm surviving.' That would work until the next time and I would talk myself through it again and again.

"I would remind myself that I had to hang in there because my husband loved me and had put so much emotional energy into all of this—supporting me—that I did NOT want to let him down! Knowing his love and support . . . all the energy he also put into uplifting me helped to keep me from giving up."

Kathie put herself through hell and survived it because of her commitment to not letting her loving, supportive husband down by collapsing under the stress of removing a toxin from her body that definitely wreaks havoc with the whole body and mind. Too many of you may be looking at these moments in a more hostile way, blaming your spouse or taking your frustrations and erratic moods out on him and her. Some of that is unavoidable, and that's why self-control and "love is ALWAYS having to say you're sorry" when you've screwed up are important.

Whining about how difficult only your suffering is ignores the reality that your suffering causes pain, concern, anxiety, and exasperation to those who love you.

When Your Pain and Fear Make You Whine at a Time Someone Needs Your Strength

There is probably no more appropriate example of this situation than a wife or mother watching her dearly beloved go off to war. Rita, a listener, has a husband leaving for Iraq and a son also deploying, but to Afghanistan. That, my friends, is a double whammy! She called because she's struggling in dealing with this emotionally, especially having three other minor children at home. She is sick to her stomach with worry—understandably— but doesn't know how to deal with these feelings and take care of the children at home and not negatively impact her deployed husband and son.

She was also not so happy that her husband of four years, a stepdad to all the children, was going to be deployed after telling her that he wouldn't be because he was with a training unit. However, they were now going to train Iraqis to fight for their own country. I reminded her that anyone in the military or associated with it knows you can't really make promises like that—especially at times of war. Anyone ought to be able to sympathize with her disappointment and fears, as well as her concerns about handling the home scene on her own for an indeterminate period of time.

Dr. Laura: So what can I do for you other than remind you that you can't whine and act moany and feel bad for yourself—remember, you have an advantage, no one is shooting at you!

Rita: (laughs) How do I cope?

Dr. Laura: You make *them* feel good; not only your warriors, but your children at home. You make them feel strong, that you're there for them and you're okay and you're taking care of things so they don't have to be worried about you. You don't make them feel bad that you're alone, you don't make them feel like they betrayed or abandoned you—you make them feel supported and you find a way to get on because you're a warrior wife and mother!

My son is deployed in a combat zone. That's the way we all have to do it. And if you have trouble with it, you go to the chaplain's office where they have counseling and support groups, wives' and mothers' groups—and you can all support each other.

Rita: You make it sound so simple.

Dr. Laura: It is, actually. It's painful and very simple. I never whine when my boy gets a chance to call; never, about anything. I would never whine to him—I'm not in combat. I haven't seen my best friend die up close and personal. Whatever I'm going through is peanuts compared to what he's going through.

Rita: This is true . . . and I will. I guess part of it is that he has to keep secrets; he can't tell me where he's at or what he's doing. So . . . I just imagine . . .

Dr. Laura: Don't. Don't go there.

Rita: How do you go on knowing that your son, Dr. Laura, is over there and you could get a phone call at any time?

That was a powerful question. I remember a time some months ago when I heard that three of our guys in my son's unit were killed in action. It was horrible, waiting for the names to be posted on that inner sanctum Web site. I figured, though, that if the phone or front door bell didn't ring . . . then the names came up and my son's name was not among them.

My reaction? I cried. I didn't cry for what you would think. I didn't cry out of relief. I cried because while one of them wasn't me, three mothers did get those phone calls. I cried for them.

Dr. Laura: There is no easy way to go through this. Just the other day I found out somebody in his unit died because he stepped on a tank mine. His unit went out and spent hours trying to collect all the small pieces of a valiant, loved, brave human being. His mother will never get to see his body. I was devastated—and I learned this just before I went out on a stage to do my one-woman show in Tucson.

I spent the day being silent and everybody was worried because I was so depressed and just barely got through the day. I went to my room and stared and tried to deal with the feelings. When I got on the stage I realized that people had come to learn something from me, that I had something of value to offer them, and you gotta do what you gotta do.

I keep in mind, Rita, what my son said to me: "I'm over here so you can do whatever you damn well please and not have to wear a burqa doing it." So I do whatever I please to honor my son and all the sons and daughters over there because they're fighting to keep the creeps back there so they won't come here.

Do not begrudge yourself having fun because your husband and son are putting their lives on the line—because they're doing so to make sure you can enjoy your life and take care of the family. If you and I don't take care of the people who rely on us, we're betraying what they're doing there to protect us.

To answer your question more succinctly, the way I get through it is to honor them. Am I upset? Yes. Am I going to fall apart and be weak? Hell no. My son didn't raise his mother to be a weenie.

And whatever you have to do, do it well so when your husband and son come back, they walk into a house where everything is going fine and everything is terrific and everybody is happy to see them and you're warm and loving. That is the best we can do for them—keep the home fires warm.

I'm sorry I gave a whole lecture; I guess it's been pent up in me.

Rita: I needed it!

Dr. Laura: Thank you, Rita. You know, you and I—we just gotta get through it as bravely as our men are getting through it.

Rita: One day at a time.

Dr. Laura: Sometimes one hour at a time.

It is extremely easy, even reflexive, to focus in on what is going on in your own mind: fears, frustrations, annoyances, and so forth. It takes maturity and compassion to try to extend the borders of your emotional preoccupations to consider what you're going through as a function of how you're needed by others.

For Better . . . and There Can Be Much Worse

I get the impression that too many folks get through their vows as quickly as possible so they can get to the reception for the drinking, eating, dancing, and collecting envelopes of money. Why do I say such a rotten thing? Because there seems to be no other explanation for the short memory concerning the vows: for better or worse.

Rachael faced this situation and dealt with it with class and honor:

"I have been a listener since I was seventeen . . . over the years I have heard time and time again pathetic wives complain and whine about their husbands. At the soccer field, at the school parking lot— mom after mom whining about their husband doing or not doing this or that or 'I want this' or 'Why can't he understand I am too tired to please him?' . . . yada, yada, yada.

"Why do I feel sorry for the hubby? Because I know this wife is not willing to sacrifice for her man.

"After only one year of marriage my husband was diagnosed with cancer. Over the next five years he would go in and out of the hospital with a deadly infection (staph-MRSA) which was a result of his cancer surgery. While battling MRSA, my hubby suffered a back injury at work, requiring major back surgery. He was flat on his back, out of work for nearly eighteen months.

"I never once thought about greener pastures. Instead, I stood by my man. I did what any decent, loving, sacrificing wife would do. Each time I nursed him back to health, swapped roles so that my husband was not rushed back to work to risk another infection.

"I never kicked my man when he was down . . . instead, I picked him up and gave him what he needed . . . lots of love. I gave and I gave and I gave.

"Dr. Laura, we just celebrated our ten-year anniversary and turning thirty at the end of the year (he just turned 31). We are young. But we know the sacrifices that must be made to keep our marriage alive. Because I was so willing to give to mine, he has given all of himself to me. My man comes home every day craving my hugs, kisses, and good loving. My man knows I am all his to have. That is what a marriage is about . . . giving to each other.

"So please tell all those whining wives to try to give a whole lot more and whine a whole lot less."

Consider yourselves told!

Now, not everyone has the ability to be so completely gung ho in the face of severe problems and sacrifice. Most of you will suffer and fret and toy with selfishness—frankly, a minimal amount of whining seems more natural to me than none.

Colette, another listener, wrote about that side of the issue. She is twenty-seven years old and has four boys (six, four, two, and five months). They found out her husband had muscular dystrophy when she was pregnant with their second son. As with most trials in life, she kept imagining this would all get better and just go away. After a while, she realized that this was just the beginning and it was going to get worse.

At times she found herself blaming her husband, his parents— or nobody in specific . . . just everybody. She would just get mad about *her* plight.

More of us can probably identify with that response.

As her husband got worse, he needed more help and it left her more and more responsible with everything around the house except for leaving the home to earn a living.

She found herself taking it all out on him emotionally and verbally.

"It has taken a lot of growing up on my part to be able to be more compassionate toward my husband, and to accept that he would be helping me if he could. He didn't ask for muscular dystrophy and he has a lot to do to deal with it himself. A lot of where I get my strength to do what is right is by listening to Dr. Laura while I wait to pick up my son."

The most important sentence in her letter is, "He didn't ask for muscular dystrophy and he has a lot to do to deal with it himself." This recognition is the epitome of empathy. Without empathy, the world is only about "me." If the world is only about "you" I guarantee you will whine yourself into loneliness and a sense of purposelessness.

Kate got a graduate course in understanding this important concept. She wrote that she started to buy into the feminist-driven mantra of "me" time. She described it as basically a sorry excuse to demand to not be held responsible or obligated to whatever the woman is taking "me" time out for.

She's an at-home mom who'd sit with her friends, also SAHMs, and lament on how they just didn't have any time to themselves. *"We had dishes to do, laundry to wash and put away, carpets to vacuum and kids to raise and play with—while our husbands just 'went off to work.'"*

Turns out that all their husbands are sailors on U.S. submarines defending their country—and not on pleasure cruises! She related actually having the nerve to say to her husband one day that she just wanted a day off, to be alone, and have "me" time.

He said to her, "I never get 'me' time."

"His saying that was a lightbulb, and I felt completely selfish and narcissistic in that very moment. I get ME time all the time. I'm free all day to come and go and do what I want with our children.

"Now I choose to see it that way. Now it's not ME time, it's U!"

Uh-oh, admitting that a state of mind is actually a choice—that's dangerous ground to the folks who revere even shifting emotions more than they do facts or the needs of others! But she's 100 percent right—it is a choice. A man called my show just yesterday to complain that his dying mother had left her small estate to his floundering sister and not him. He was angry that his mom would "reward" (his word) his errant sister, and he was hurt that his mom would not want to "reward" him for being the good son.

Trust me, this man was very upset. I just immediately launched into "You know, I'm kind of surprised you're even upset. When your mother decided to apportion her assets in the way you described, it was a definite compliment to you. She recognizes that you are a strong and accomplished man and can handle life well. She recognizes that your sister is none of that, and she has to rescue her one last time even after death."

He sounded immediately surprised and confused. I repeated myself so that I would overwhelm any of his defenses against the good-news view of his situation.

Finally he sounded pleased. Why? He *chose* to accept another worldview outside of himself. No more whining, just pleasure and a sense of being special to his mother—by *not* getting the cash.

Blessings from the Pits of Hell

Hell may sound like a strange place to imagine receiving blessings—but it is probably one of the best sources of them.

In my twenties I was a biology teacher in a four-year college run by a well-known order of nuns. I was asked to give a presentation on . . . I don't remember . . . but somewhere in the talk I really blew it. I said something to the effect that "suffering has no positive place in life." Most of the nuns walked out of the auditorium.

I had a lot to learn.

And I had to do it through suffering myself and through the words of those who suffered. Sharon was one of my lessons:

"This week I am facing my fourth major abdominal operation related to ovarian cancer. When I knew I would need this fourth operation, I felt that I did not want to relive all the physical pain and suffering I had experienced in the course of the prior treatments and operations."

Understandably, Sharon couldn't see the cancer center as a place of healing, a place that had saved her life; she saw it only as hell . . . a place of pain. A friend suggested to her that when she was in the hospital she pray for the other people there who are also suffering and in pain. She decided to make it her goal to be kind to each person she encountered during her time there: the doctors, nurses, techs, and the cleaning people.

"I try to focus not on the pain of the past, but on small ways I can focus on others. The emotional pain is already lifting in a way I could not have imagined."

On a more minor level, let's talk about the pain of childbirth. In preparation for labor, I took the courses in breathing and focusing. The only positive thing I have to say about this training is that they tell you not to scream. Perhaps they tell you that because it upsets the doctors, nurses, and other patients. I'm sure it does—but that isn't the main point. The main point is that when you are in pain, whether physical and/or emotional, screaming (and whining) accentuates the pain and brings your whole focus on the pain. The pain becomes you and you are reduced to being pain—and *a* pain if it goes on too long!

We are human beings and can rise above our circumstances to be and do better.

No Way Out?

I hate to admit this, but there are times I'm not sure that someone I'm helping can or will improve. Some folks are way too wedded to their inner portrayal of life; others are so damaged that they can barely function, much less risk challenge and change. However, I always act as though there is hope. My attitude being negative will add only one more limitation to someone's already sad soul.

I took a call from DeAnna that fits this general description. She is forty-one years old, single, no children, and told me that for many years she has had a pretty serious mental condition and is taking medication under a doctor's care.

DeAnna: Severe depression. I was hospitalized a few years back . . . in and out of hospitals, and my issue with this is that, over the years, the people that I really depend on, who were my friends, because of my actions and because of my illness, I've lost just about all of them. I'm pretty much alone.

Dr. Laura: Yeah, sometimes people do get worn out.

DeAnna: Yeah, I guess they do. I can't blame them. I've

listened to you, as I've said, for many years, and I know that folks aren't looking for folks who are messed up. I try my best not to be—but I don't know what I can offer.

At this point I had to take a commercial break. An interruption is not always a bad thing; in fact I value it as time to assess the situation and time for the caller to calmly react to all that's gone on. I had the feeling that her negativity and identity as a sad person were her treasure—and one she would not readily give up. The alternative would be too scary. She'd feel naked in the world without cloaking herself in her own sympathy. I just knew I couldn't go there if there was any hope for growth.

So I try to come in through the basement!

Dr. Laura: I see that you have serious problems of being a depressed person, of looking at the world negatively, assuming that you're not going to be loved and valued, assuming you're not going to be well taken care of . . . it's such an ingrained habit for you that . . . I don't know . . . perhaps we should make the assumption that we can't make a big dent in it.

DeAnna: Okay.

Do you see how readily she accepted the negative? That actually heartened me that I was on the right track. If I attacked the depression, she'd get defensive to protect it and herself. I told her she gets to keep it, and she relaxed.

Dr. Laura: However, there are always alternatives. Do you realize that there are kids out there more negative than you?

DeAnna: I didn't realize that . . . no.

Dr. Laura: And I'm thinking that even though we maybe can't fix you, that you have such incredible insight into what this feels like and how the behavioral patterns become so rigid that it's hard to stop them, that you might be of great benefit to kids in emotional need.

DeAnna: (excited voice) I never thought of that! Okay.

Dr. Laura: So you could help them not get to *your* point in life.

DeAnna: Okay. How do I go about doing that?

I explained some of the resources available, including a bit of counseling training in a community college, volunteer programs, and such.

Dr. Laura: So your life, while we may not be able to make it perfect for you—your life could become the catalyst to help kids who are suffering like you have. Wouldn't that be a good use of your life? And your pain?

DeAnna: Oh, it sure would. It really, really would.

Dr. Laura: I think you could do this. I think you could make a great difference in kids' lives.

DeAnna: I really would like to think that I could. I sure would give it my best shot.

Dr. Laura: And what you'd get back from them is seeing them do better than you . . . because somebody like you intervened for them, where nobody intervened like that for you.

DeAnna: (sounding enthused) Wouldn't that be great?!

Dr. Laura: (softly) Yeah. It would make all your suffering worth it.

What I appreciated about this call is that suffering can sometimes be the starting point for blessings for others! DeAnna found a way to protect her ongoing sad identity while discovering that she had something to offer that would make people not turn away from her anymore. In fact, her sadness, her great understanding of sadness, *is* the healing factor.

Closing Sentiment

I recently took a call from an adult married daughter who wanted to give her dad permission to start dating, since he was lonely because her mom was in the last stages of Alzheimer's. I remarked that although she couldn't recognize him, he knew who she was and vows were still operative, as Alzheimer's was obviously the "worse" part of the "better or worse" part of the wedding promises. The whining about not having life the way you'd like it makes so many people sink to a very low level.

Happily, the very next day a listener wrote me about her dear grandfather. After celebrating their sixtieth anniversary, Grandma was diagnosed with Alzheimer's. Grandpa was her sole caregiver for many years—even being with her the whole day when she needed to be sent to a nursing home. On many occasions, her grandfather would pull out his wallet and show off the old black-and-white photo of her grandmother and him on their wedding day.

"My grandpa would point to it and say, 'You see that, there is my little sweetheart.' My grandfather would spend his days in a nursing home with a wife who no longer recognized him because he still saw her as his 'little sweetheart.'

"After my grandmother passed, the nurses at the nursing home and his two daughters were praising him for being so good to my grandmother. His answer? 'It was nothing, because you see, I once stood before a judge and made a vow to love through good times and bad. The way I see it, we had a lot, a lot, of good times; these past few years were just the bad.'

"Not only was my grandpa an example to his children, but an example to his grand- and great-grandchildren. We lost my grandpa two years ago, but his example of making vows and keeping them still lives."

Whining doesn't inspire generation after generation—does it?

CHAPTER 7

Start Living

"I cannot stress enough the importance of getting 'fed up' to make a change! I was single, alone, bored, and feeling like I didn't matter to anyone except my mom and my dog . . . and they were required to love me.

"I heard Dr. Laura talking one day about how 'if you don't like your life . . . stop whining . . . change it! Do whatever it takes to make that happen . . . no matter how difficult . . . do it.'

"So I did!

"I adopted two at-risk teenage girls and my life has never been fuller; also crazy, hectic, and at times so overwhelming that I can't see straight, but it is definitely full. And I feel like I am making a difference in someone else's life, thinking outside of myself, and learning how to put another human being's needs and feelings above my own. That may sound easy, but for a whiny, spoiled rotten brat, it was hard! To this day, at times, it is still hard—but it is worth it.

"I owe my new life to Dr. L's kick in the butt."

—TRISH, A LISTENER

Consider this chapter a kind of inspirational "kick in the butt." I can't really present you with a complete compendium of recipes for success in life for every situation you might be in. But what I can do is share the stories of people who have struggled with demons from within and without, and give their testimonies as to how and why they stopped whining and started living. These stories are in no order of so-called importance, as I see every journey as equally important. I'm going to start though with the letter that sounded the simplest in its clarity—yet dealt with the most profound of issues: life and death.

I'm Going to Die Anyway

Angela is going to die—sooner rather than later. Four years ago, at forty-seven, she was diagnosed with stage I rectal cancer. It was removed and she was told that there was a 90 percent chance it would not recur. She didn't smoke, she rarely had alcohol, and was a healthy, active mother of four. She went into understandable shock, but believed she had beaten it.

Almost a year and half later, it was back. After seven hours of surgery she ended up with a permanent colostomy, no bladder function for six weeks, radiation burns to her vagina preventing intercourse as well as minimizing sensitivity, muscle weakness from the chemo, instant menopause, and thirty extra pounds from the changes to her metabolism and hormones.

Her family stood by her suffering through a month of radiation, six months of chemo, nausea, and problems with memory and speech. They all thought they got through it.

No such luck. It is now back in her lung. If she does nothing, she has a 50 percent chance of living for one more year. If she has a painful surgery, she gets a 30 percent chance of living five more years—with more debilitating treatments. Her doctors agree that all they can do is make her feel worse and prolong that kind of quality of life.

> *"After long talks with my husband and children (15, 22, 24, 26), we all agreed that we would rather have me here and feeling decent for a few [less years than sick from chemo for longer] (I really never felt bad from the cancer, just the treatments). . . ."*

I'm sure Angela has spent some time cursing the fates that brought her to this place, but I am particularly moved by her decision to use the precious time she has for the benefit of her family and their mutual closeness. She certainly is looking at this as the glass half full.

I remember reading somewhere a long time ago that one of Satan's plans is to make human beings believe they have all the time in the world because then they worry less about morals and values and more about instant gratification. Youth feels immortal; middle age knows it's not. However, people confronting life-threatening illnesses seem to express a profound affection for every moment available, albeit sometimes only after a bout with anger and depression.

At these times you can curse the coming darkness or praise the available light. I am always deeply moved by people who embrace the latter. It's all we have actually, those moments of life with those who matter.

Hitting the Road . . . Finally

I get way too many calls from women with serious and scary complaints about their men: so obsessive-compulsive that kids can't make a peep when Dad's home, or physically violent with or without alcohol or drugs. When I suggest the obvious "Get out of Dodge," that's when the excuses start flowing: "I want my kids to have a dad," "I have nowhere to go," "He's not always this bad," "He promised he'd change," and on and on.

One woman, Ronie, wrote me back after such a conversation with me on my radio program about her life with an abusive husband:

"I've been doing a lot of thinking about my life and the bad marriage I'm in after our phone conversation last week which upset me. I've come to realize that no phone call, no advice from friends or family

is going to 'fix' my situation. I'm the only one that can change things.

"I just wanted you to know that I'm leaving him and moving out. Not just for myself but so my daughter has a chance someday at a healthy relationship. I don't want her growing up thinking this is okay and normal. I love you, Dr. Laura—you help me so much every day. Yes, you can really be hard on people sometimes—but I think that's what we need to gain strength and see the truth.

"'Accept the things we cannot change and have the courage to change the things we can. And the wisdom to know the difference.' (AA serenity prayer) Wow. So true."

The reason Ronie had such a problem with our radio conversation was precisely what she ended up doing: taking personal responsibility for her situation versus being the victim, martyr, or confused (I always love when people throw this one at me)—which is exactly what I exhorted her to do.

Too many people whine as though whining had power. Well, it does, to a certain limited extent. It blows off steam and it gets solicitousness from others . . . for a while. It is like a salve on a burn: feels good for a while and then, bam, the pain is back with a fury.

Ronie did what always has to be done: an action of courage which makes you vulnerable and uncomfortable but gives you the only opportunity to jump-start a reasonable life again.

Pity Party Folks Fail

As if to prove my point, I received this right-on-the-point letter from Lela:

"I remember at a much younger age 'talking, whining, rehashing, complaining and suffering,' and how little impact these traits had on what was going on. It kept me down and wallowing with the masses in their mire. I noticed that those that didn't participate in the 'pity party' were successful, smiling, and looked much younger than their years.

"When I slowly gravitated toward the 'other group,' I noticed their traits rubbed off on me; my financial woes started fading away and I had less stress on my shoulders. The people I attracted were more kind and more willing to mentor me. I started smiling more often and people weren't intimidated by me anymore. My business began flourishing. I was less threatened by others' success; in fact, I could even ask for advice and get it! Today I am surrounded by successful and happy people and am able to mentor new young people who show promise and eagerness to be successful, happy people."

Yes, friends, this is a "birds of a feather" moment. It is not surprising that AA recommends that its members not hang with the old friends with the bad behaviors. It is not paranoid for parents to be concerned about the direction their children are headed when their friends are the kids who don't study but do wreak havoc. It is also not surprising when a husband or wife gets concerned when his or her spouse begins spending time with single folks who stay out and party. Who you choose to spend your time with and consider important in your life for companionship and feedback is pretty much a simple assessment of what you value and the identity you wish to give yourself.

When you gravitate toward negativity, it reinforces the negativity. When you pull yourself—albeit kicking and screaming on the inside—toward the more difficult concept of living life, it brings you toward a more hopeful and productive state of mind and being. So-called friends inhabiting your same murky pond are never going to challenge that strong, healthy part of you into swimming ashore; they wouldn't want to be alone, nor would they want to challenge themselves. Therefore, get ready for their undermining of your progress. That's why it is a far, far better thing you'd do to find new friends . . . even if it means you are alone for some time. If you can't be alone with yourself, who do you imagine would volunteer for that job?

I See the Future . . . Arrgghh!

Rhonda wrote:

"This is going to start off like so many other letters to you. It used to tick me off to no end when you'd refuse to offer someone help out of an impossible situation. I would get so mad at you for telling some young woman that she had messed up her life so badly that there was no way to fix it . . . she'd have to endure and make the best of it.

"Then one day on my way to work, it hit me. I was shacking up with the male who was way too old for me—and alcoholic! I looked into my future and saw me picking up the phone to call you while a kid or two were at my ankles, complaining (and whining) that I didn't love my controlling boyfriend. You were talking to me when you didn't answer the unfixable problem. You were showing me the path that I was headed down.

"That night I told my shack-up honey I was moving out that weekend. I did just that. I moved into my very small car and stored

my stuff. I lived that way for three months until I found a job near
my mom. I moved home and paid off all of my bills.

"I became a person who I respected.

"Now I have a wonderful husband, two marvelous kids, and a
home of our own. I can never thank you enough for not answering
questions. You gave me a life that I had no idea I could have."

What struck me the most about this letter is that it spoke
directly to the title of this book . . . except that Rhonda was
wisely preemptive! She knew she'd end up whining and whining
and that I'd tell her something like, "Sorry, with two kids,
you have to—for their well-being—endure the best you can to
provide them some stability. This can't be fixed—too late. It must
be endured."

The point of documenting all these calls and letters is to give
you enough scenarios that one might strike you as way too close to
home; and better still, before it becomes "impossible." For some of
you, then is now. You are already whining and feeling perpetually
trapped . . . yet the whining state is just about the only condition
you imagine is possible. Let me repeat an important concept:
enduring. What we can't change (or fix) must be endured. That
means the whining stops because you set your mind, heart, and
soul to how to make the best out of a situation you'd rather not be
in . . . but it is too late. You must be polite, nice, helpful, positive,
kind, patient; you know, some of that actually is a potent salve to
make the unendurable even pleasant. And enough of that might
change the situation completely—and for the better.

Hey . . . I'm Not Crazy . . .
Am I or Could I Become Crazy?

One of my listeners, Dee, wrote about being "wrongly" sent to a psych ward. After being overmedicated she decided to take her own life.

> *"It was probably the best thing for me because it was in there that I realized if I didn't help myself at twenty-five and start doing what needed to be done, I would have wound up where these people were: the point of no return. It is not so much that being there helped me; just that being there made me see that if I keep on being the way I am (isolated, negative, wallowing in poor me mode) I would drive myself crazy and really need to be in the psych ward. Luckily, it took only forty-eight hours to realize that I didn't have to live like that, and another five days for the doctors to decide I wasn't a threat to myself anymore."*

I frankly get really impressed with people like Dee. She brought herself back from the edge, and that is no small feat. Perhaps this is a situation that some people point to when they say, "You have to hit rock bottom before you get awakened to the reality of where your life is headed." It must seem strange to some of you to imagine that you could have such a moment of clarity as Dee had in the mental hospital, and jettison yourself out of that desperate space in your mind. The change doesn't happen in the same flash as the epiphany. That is where grit and help come in. But none of that matters unless you're committed to the discomfort of making new decisions, which are usually recognized in their value by how difficult they are to face.

You Have the Power!

I get so many calls with whining complaints about the moodiness of one's spouse. Generally, the spouse's unpleasant state of mind is met with frustration, anger, and impatience, after being understanding and trying to talk the person out of the mood doesn't work.

Valerie, a *good* listener to the program, knew exactly what to do to rescue the moment in her home. Their family-run business was going through some difficult times, and her husband had to take on a huge workload that he'd been previously sharing with another employee. It involved nine to ten hours of stop-and-go city driving that, in addition to the obvious mental stress, messed up his back. He had to do this to pay their bills and keep them afloat.

He called her midafternoon one day and was very testy and grouchy. Finally he apologized for his ill-temper and said it was just that he hadn't eaten lunch. He has such a workload on his back that he didn't want to stop and take the time to get lunch.

"I was pissed at first. How dare he do this to himself and then take it out on me. But since he had apologized so sweetly, I got over it quickly. But the next day it happened again.

"I then had a Dr. Laura Moment and said to myself, 'If the man doesn't have time to stop and get some lunch, well then, I'll just fix it for him!' So Sunday night, I made him a big batch of egg salad and baked a yummy spice bread. Monday morning he took sandwiches and Doritos and was a happy man in the afternoon! He was overcarbed . . . but no more grouchy stuff. He has taken his

lunch all this week and has been great. It takes over five minutes to fix, and either saves from five to seven dollars a day . . . or five hours of aggravation.

"Thank you for your voice in my head, reminding me to give him the gift of understanding, and look for a solution rather than nurse hurt (whiny) feelings. I'm somewhat proud of myself."

I'm obviously very proud of Valerie for having the compassion and common sense to look for the real problem: not hurt feelings, not insensitivity, not selfishness, not out-of-control anger issues . . . simply hunger. She left her own emotional dominion to realize what the problem was and solved it simply. Win-win.

Learn to Shut Up!

Whew! That's quite an inflammatory concept. Nonetheless, when you feel very much like sitting and whining about your lot in life . . . shut up instead! Get up and do your job, no matter how overwhelmed you feel by your own desire to bitch, bitch, and bitch some more. Lila sent me a letter that started out with that revelation. She then ended up suggesting two more ideas:

1. Serve other people . . . instead of trying to get them to take care of poor little me.

2. Practice being kind . . . instead of having constant expectations and disappointments about what I'd get from them.

Considering number 1: I'm sure you have all sorts of talents that could be put to good use to benefit others. If you can sing, entertain folks in homes for the aged or in church. If you can do crafts, work at a kid's camp or the YMCA; volunteer at a hospital to read. There is no end to where your talents could blossom and make people happy, leaving you feeling quite purposeful and necessary on the face of the earth. Practicing kindness is usually the last thing a whiny person feels like doing. Nonetheless, the more you behave loving and patient, the more natural it begins to feel, the better you begin to feel and the better people feel about you.

It isn't quick and it isn't easy, but it can be done.

Drop the Blaming

It is sooooo easy to blame your situation, life experience, coworkers, parents, pimples, moon spots, spouses, or bad luck for what is, in truth, your own lack of effort, courage, patience, commitment, or plain common sense. The obviously good part of blaming is that it gets you off the hook from being responsible— and without having responsibility, you don't have to make any changes in yourself or make apologies and redress with anyone else.

Mike admitted to this when he wrote:

"I look back and realized I blamed situations on 'things/scenarios' rather than say, 'Okay, it is what it is NOW. How can I pick up the pieces and place ownership on it?' Once I own this, I control the outcome from that point on.

"The downside, you are responsible for whatever 'this' is. The 'victim' side wants to do nothing and blame rather than fix and work hard. My dad was right when he said, 'Nothing is free—and if you don't work hard for it, you don't deserve it.'"

Of course there are certain obstacles and choices other people make that you will have no control over. However, you choose what your actions and decisions will be from that point on. There are no real excuses for not doing the right thing.

Think of Three Nice Things to Say

When I was in private practice, I realized early on that couples in and out of therapy spent communication time ragging on each other. It seemed obvious to me that this approach never brought the best out of anybody, including affection and the dropping of defenses. I would ask family members in family therapy to start each session going around the room coming up with just one nice thing to say about each and every member of the family. It was amazing to see how quickly the mood changed from petty rage into laughter and tears. I would ask married couples to list three nice things about the other person even now that the relationship was in trouble. It was lovely to watch how soft each became during this sharing time.

I have also suggested that parents use this with squabbling kids. Usually the first responses will be banal: "You look good in that shirt." At some point, it will slip into the kids trying hard to make each other laugh. Be careful with this technique. It is so much fun your kids might want to squabble more!

The next time you feel so terribly angry with your spouse that you can barely stand him or her . . . start listing two to four really nice things about him/her. You will come to first balance all the emotions; and then your spouse will likely shift to be more appreciative and loving.

This way of thinking and behaving is emphasized in Amy's letter:

"The power of life and death is in the tongue, and mine was very negative. I spoke negative words to my husband, children and friends. The damage done to myself and my family was evident in our attitudes.

"Negative self-talk also did a lot of damage to my goals and dreams. I believed for so long what I told myself: that I was ugly, fat, unlovable, stupid, unlikable, etc.

"Now, because the Lord led many Christian friends into my life, and many wonderful books to teach me how to live and speak positively, I have a lot of positive fruit in my life. I speak blessings to and about my husband and children, I don't gossip, I'm an agent of positive conversation with friends, and I consistently work on positive self-talk and realizing that I am a child of God, and that He loves me.

"Possibly the greatest reason for my new attitude is that when given the tools for a life of freedom from a damaging tongue, I MADE THE DECISION TO CHANGE, and then manage that decision every day."

You know, I read all these letters and the common denominator is always that the individual made a choice. That sounds so mundane, I know, but think about it: how many times have you felt your emotions were out of control, that there was nothing you could really do to effect change in your life, even that you have behavioral addictions (instead of repetitive, habitual bad choices)?

Deciding to make a choice is the decision to become supremely human. Lower animals run largely on instinct. What makes humans so special is the ability to reason and make choices. That's your power. Use it.

I Want It . . . Now!

A number of people call my radio program every day to whine about how impossible it is for them to resist some food and/or get motivated to exercise. Erin's letter indicated that when she was twenty-nine, she was five feet two inches and weighed 253 pounds! Her boyfriend kept breaking off with her because, in her words, he loved her but "didn't want to be married to a slug." She had been carefree her whole life—aka nondisciplined—about food choices and physical activity, caring mostly about instant gratification rather than what she was doing to herself.

Giving up the instant gratification for long-term gain is not easy because the decision to forgo the moment is one thing, but handling the day-to-day losses, frustrations, and temptations is a stress and a challenge of massive proportions.

Yet again, it all starts with a choice.

Erin's attachment to instant gratification had to do with making herself feel better because of coming from the loss of an intact home, financial issues, and more. Instead of either pushing those feelings aside or displacing them with noble activities, people find it way too easy to simply make themselves feel better—for that moment—and pay the larger price (obesity) down the line.

Erin had the incentive because of her fiancé: *"I have learned that the work is MINE to do. I have to regain my health and show this great guy—and he is a good man—that I care enough about my life to be the gift that he truly deserves."*

I couldn't be more excited about her last sentence if I had written it myself! That is so important a concept: if you don't care enough about yourself to make yourself your best self, why should anyone else value you? You are the leader of that pack!

Let's Pretend

I've often told people whining about their marriages or workplace dynamics to behave as if they were happy and thought well about the other person. Specifically I would say to a spouse, "Behave *as if* you loved him/her with every fiber of your being." You can change love to respect for a coworker. You don't have to tell me that doing this can sometimes be so difficult to imagine, much less do, that you think you might explode.

Do what Dawn did:

"I suffer from occasional depression, although I've been able to control it with journaling, exercise, and meds. The last six months have been hell for me. My father died, I had a hysterectomy, my son and mother had surgery, and I have a stressful job.

"Needless to say I've been feeling sorry for myself. On Father's Day I woke up VERY depressed. I just wanted to dig a hole somewhere and hide from the world.

"I freaked out making breakfast because my fifteen-month-old and four-year-old were underfoot and my husband just muttered unhappily, 'Happy Father's Day.'

"I went outside and reflected. The one word that came to mind (from your radio show) was 'pretend.' I DID NOT feel like being a good wife or mother today. I walked back into the house LIKE I WAS a new woman, even though I still felt like hiding.

"The reason I'm writing this is because you saved our day. I'm writing this as my children are napping (tired from swimming all day), my husband is watching NASCAR and getting ready to go fishing, and all is well and peaceful because I decided to pretend!"

So even before you have a change of mind or heart—you can behave as though you have had a change of mind or heart. Funny thing, it usually makes you feel a change in mind and heart.

Physical Pain Go Away . . . Don't Come Back Some Other Day

There are certain medical conditions that won't necessarily go away. Lupus is one of them. Everyone with lupus has a different story, depending on the type of lupus and the person's own genetics and state of health. Deon was diagnosed with lupus almost three decades ago. She spends her life constantly feeling as though she has the flu. It used to—and quite understandably so—make her feel sorry for herself. However, that state of mind was consuming her. She worked with her doctors, and took all the appropriate medications.

She then decided to distract her mind from her pain by living life—by doing.

"I got busy with my kids, extended family, running my business, and keeping my mind on the other things. It worked! When I'm busy I don't notice the ache. In the evenings, when I slow down, I start feeling the pain and know it is time for my meds, relaxation, pajamas, and a diet Coke.

"The worst times were when I had a lupus flare when my body hurt so bad that two or three times over the twenty-nine years I didn't care if I died. Now I believe that because I have perfect children and a perfect husband that I can surely handle this annoying health challenge."

The Booze or My Children?

It is such a lovely thing to read or hear that people make the best of a difficult situation for the benefit of others. That compassion feeds back with more peace in your own soul and psyche. Another listener, Tom, a divorced parent, gave up drinking because:

"The best thing in the world is being able to be there for my boys. I think every day what if—what if something was to happen to one of my boys and I couldn't be there to help them because I was drunk. What if I was drunk and couldn't teach them how to grow up to be a man and stand on their own two feet. The choice is easy if you think about it."

I'll Do Anything for My Kids

Linda decided that she'd stay in what she thought was a lousy marriage for the sake of her kids. That's very noble and self-sacrificing. But it is not enough to just be there, you have to give of yourself while you're there—something besides whining. She felt her husband had many faults and that they differed greatly in their opinions on how to do things. She found herself getting frustrated with him and found it harder and harder to feel any kind of love or respect for him.

She decided to stay in a loveless marriage so her children could have an intact home. Then, listening to my program, she realized that if she was willing to do ANYTHING for her children, then she should also be willing to make her marriage a LOVING marriage for them too, since children have a right and a need to having loving parents who care for each other. At that point she realized she needed an attitude change. She admitted to herself the most important fact: that she contributed to the failures in her marriage just as much as her husband.

She started looking for ways that her husband contributed to their family, instead of looking for, or only noticing, the things her husband did "wrong." She started being affectionate with him—even though in the beginning she had very little true desire to do so. She began actually listening to his advice and opinions, instead of becoming instantly defensive. She did what she could to nurture and strengthen him, even though for some period of time it was not reciprocated, probably because of all the hurt he'd experienced from her rejection.

Through doing these deeds, she discovered that he was really a good man who loved his children and his wife.

"I found that he was needing to be emotionally fed just as much as I. What a loss I had been creating for myself and my children all these years because of my pridefulness and stubbornness. I was able to turn things around for our family—just in the nick of time! HE was ready to begin divorce proceedings. My attitude change was enough to give our marriage one more chance.

"Even now, our marriage is not perfect and we BOTH still need to work on a lot of things! We still have differences that come up, but we are working TOGETHER to resolve our issues because we love our family and realized that we still love each other. Loving and supporting each other is the greatest gift we can give our children."

Look at what Linda was willing to admit to: "pridefulness and stubbornness." Other contributors have brought up other negative dimensions such as selfishness and insensitivity. While it is really uncomfortable and embarrassing to own up to such behaviors and thought patterns, what a relief it is at the same time! Once you acknowledge the roadblocks to your happiness, you can drive around them to lovelier territories. Whining is generally about serving and protecting the "self." Yet, ironically, the self is best served by the love and admiration of others who are so very grateful for your openness, willingness to accept responsibility, and—very important—compassion for their humanness that gives evidence through glitches in behavior and demeanor.

Forget the "aha, I gotcha" moments in which you prove your superiority or victimhood. Remember that giving, giving, giving is the best way to receive the blessings we all hope, dream, and pray for that make life worth living.

Closing Sentiment

In *The Proper Care and Feeding of Marriage* I talk about the 15 Minute Rule that came up during a call from a woman complaining that her husband had spent the last nine years having fifteen-minute sessions of sexual intimacy in his car with a co-worker. I wondered aloud how the last nine years would have been different had the caller spent fifteen minutes every morning having passionate sex with her husband before he left the home.

For months I received letters from folks invoking the 15 Minute Rule in their marriages. Joe had a different take, one very appropriate to our subject, whining less and living more:

"I woke up early the other morning, and in the dark before my wife woke up, I thought of all the response the '15 minute' story generated. It occurred to me that fifteen minutes first thing in the morning would be good for a lot of the neglected areas of my life.

"What if I spent fifteen minutes every morning exercising or walking? I bet I'd feel a lot better.

"What if I spent the first fifteen minutes at work doing something that would improve my skills or qualifications, and not just despamming my inbox?

"What if I took fifteen minutes for one-on-one time every day with each of my children?

"Finally, what if I spent fifteen minutes in the morning reading scriptures, meditating, or praying?

"Even though I'm busy, I think there is more than enough time in my day usually used for far less worthy activities that could be 'reassigned' if I just make the important stuff first priority.

"And since my wife doesn't apparently know about '15 minutes' of lovin' every morning . . . yet . . . I have some days to get started on one or two of these other things!"

When you put it that way, Joe, it seems like a series of fifteen-minute commitments will create a lot of accomplishments, good feeling, and much less whining about what you can never get to because you're just too busy, too tired, too this and too that.

Living life is about action: courageous, benevolent, worthy, wise, and productive *action*.

Whining is a form of despair. In the words of Rabbi Menachem Schneerson: "Despair is a cheap excuse for avoiding one's purpose in life. And a sense of purpose is the best way to avoid despair."

In a nutshell, when you spend your time whining, justified or not, you lose time living. Don't make that trade-off. Make the story of your life an inspiration to the generations.

Postscript

My final sentiments are expressed so well in this letter from Kathy:

"I am a fairly new listener to the Dr. Laura program, but have already put into play something you emphasize to callers almost daily: STOP WHINING. I never realized how much we whine and want to make big deals out of things that aren't.

"The world, and everyone in it that we touch, are not out to hurt us. No wonder we fail at relationships. In the short time that I've made this conscious effort to knock it off, I have been amazed at the happiness that has resulted. And, believe it or not, it wasn't that hard to do.

"Folks, listen up! Be happy. Stop looking for the dark cloud. I think we'll live longer and definitely make those around us happier too."

And as Jack, a pilot for the Air Force and a major airline, wrote so succinctly:

"If the grass is greener on the other side, water your own damn lawn."

And now, my friends, STOP WHINING AND START LIVING!

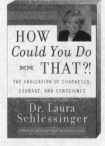